St. Paul and Epicurus

BY NORMAN WENTWORTH DeWITT

# ST. PAUL

*and*

# EPICURUS

UNIVERSITY OF MINNESOTA PRESS · MINNEAPOLIS

PRINTED AT LUND PRESS, INC., MINNEAPOLIS

*Library of Congress Catalog Card Number: 54-12314*

PUBLISHED IN GREAT BRITAIN, INDIA, AND PAKISTAN BY
GEOFFREY CUMBERLEGE: OXFORD UNIVERSITY PRESS, LONDON, BOMBAY, AND KARACHI

# PREFACE

THE present study is a sequel to the author's *Epicurus and His Philosophy* and it aims at making good the thesis there enunciated that Epicureanism functioned as a bridge of transition from Greek philosophy to the Christian religion. It is hoped by this means to have opened up a new window on the New Testament, a window walled up by prejudice long centuries ago.

This prejudice had its root in exasperation over the theology of Epicurus, which repudiated belief in miracles, prophecy, divine providence, and immortality. Epicurus was consequently denounced as an atheist, which he was not.

Joined with this exasperating theology was an alluring body of ethical doctrine, neatly organized and attractively presented. Unluckily, however, part of the lure of the ethic consisted in analyzing happiness to consist of the memory of pleasures past, the enjoyment of pleasures present, and the hope of pleasures to come. This espousal of pleasure as the chief good of life gave excuse for denouncing Epicurus as a sensualist, which he was not. His pleasures were not the pleasures of the flesh.

Nevertheless the merit of this ethic was so superior and so widely acknowledged that Paul had no alternative but to adopt it and bless it with the new sanction of religion, though to admit his indebtedness to the alleged atheist and sensualist was inconceivable. Epicurus was consequently consigned to anonymity.

When once this screen of anonymity has been penetrated, we shall find that the most beloved devotional readings in the Epistles of Paul exhibit the greatest influence of the friendly Epicurus. An example is

v

the illustrious hymn to love in First Corinthians 13. The philosophy of love or friendship had created a climate of feeling favorable to the acceptance of the religion of love. Epicurus had also established a cult of peace, whether peace of mind or peace among men, long before Paul preached "the gospel of peace" and "the God of peace."

Epicurus had set the fashion for expounding doctrine in the form of an epistle. One of these writings bore the title *To the Friends in Asia* and was in circulation for three centuries before Paul composed his Epistle with the inscription *To the Saints Which Are in Ephesus.*

Long before the congregations organized by Paul began to assemble in private houses to perpetuate the memory of Jesus the Christ, innumerable colonies of the disciples of Epicurus had been accustomed to meet in private houses to perpetuate the memory of their founder, whom they revered as the discoverer of truth and a savior. Epicurus, according to the records, had so ordered it, just as we are informed that Jesus did.

The ability to follow the trail of these hidden parallelisms and to spot the unacknowledged adaptations of Epicurean teachings in the writings of Paul is the sole advantage to be claimed by the author of this study over other scholars. The process of detection, when once the clues have been identified, will not be difficult; one discovery will ease the way to another and in the end the total number of appropriated teachings may prove to be astonishing.

Among the immediate rewards will be more precise translations and occasionally for the first time correct translations.

It was the first intention of the author to entitle this study *Epicurus and the New Testament* but it speedily became apparent that the Pauline writings called for treatment apart from the Gospels.

The division into chapters under the names of the Epistles has resulted in a moderate amount of repetition, for which no apology seems necessary. The objective has been discovery and instruction, not entertainment.

As a last word the author disavows all claim to have made a definitive investigation. He will be content with the hope of having made a definite breach in the ancient wall of prejudice and anonymity. To the work yet to be done in this line of research there is no near limit.

This limit is the farther removed for several reasons. The treatment accorded to Epicurus in histories of philosophy is perfunctory and marred at its best by the inveterate omissions, errors, and prejudices. As for the source materials, even good university libraries may be ill supplied with them; certain items have been long out of print; others have never been translated; many are fragmentary and yield their data only to a diligent and practiced scholar. Even a willing and competent researcher would do well after a year's study to feel capable of handling his sources with facility.

The human factor must also be reckoned with; the philosophy of Epicurus was animated by a characteristic spirit, genial and reasonable and yet resolute, and to capture this spirit will demand a change of attitude, which is not to be accomplished overnight.

In the present study all questions of scholarship concerning the authenticity of certain Epistles have been ignored as unessential to the problem of Epicurean influence. In general the endeavor has been made to hold the exposition at the level of the educated layman, for whom the source material would neither be available nor usable. Those readers who will find profit in footnotes are referred to the preceding volume, *Epicurus and His Philosophy*.

Thanks are due to a former pupil, Miss E. Marguerite Baker, who generously volunteered to help in the preparation of the manuscript; to a capable colleague, Dr. W. E. Staples, who gave advice on Hebrew thought and literature; and to Professor Arthur Stanley Pease of Harvard University, whose candid criticisms on matters of Epicureanism have always merited respect.

N. W. D.

*143 Eleventh Street*
*Lincoln, Illinois*
*August 1954*

# CONTENTS

St. Paul and Epicurus

# EPICURUS

## Life and Teachings

Eₚɪᴄᴜʀᴜs, although an Athenian citizen by birth, was neither born nor raised in Athens but on the island of Samos not far from Ephesus. The fact is significant: he grew up entirely free from the political obsession that plagued the Athenians of Athens. He favored a minimum of government control and a maximum of individual freedom, while Plato, an Athenian of Athens, fathered the highly regimented state with a minimum of individual freedom and a maximum of government control.

These two ideals are still competitors in our modern world. The open type of society which was sponsored by Epicurus has allied itself with Christianity. The closed type of society which was sponsored by Plato has taken its stand against religion.

The year of Epicurus' birth was 341 B.C. This date will take on significance if it be recalled that Plato was then seven years in his grave and only seven years were to elapse before Alexander should set out on his momentous career of conquest. Thus the lifetime of Epicurus fell squarely in the interval of transition between the localized and introvert culture of ancient Greece and the cosmopolitan and extrovert culture of the so-called Hellenistic age.

In respect of social class Epicurus belonged to the educated poor; his father was a schoolmaster. This too is significant; it placed a social discount upon his philosophy, because schoolmasters enjoyed little esteem in the ancient world, even among the cultured Greeks. Intellectual aristocrats, including those who aspired to be thought of this class, preferred Platonism. Cicero once wrote in a snobbish mood: "I would prefer to agree with Plato and be wrong rather than to agree

3

with Epicurus and be right." Epicureanism was destined to flourish best among the thrifty and intelligent middle classes, the same levels of society to which Paul addressed his message.

## Education

An incident that has been recorded from the school days of Epicurus informs us of his precocity and his independent spirit. The teacher was dictating a line of poetry that ran, "Verily first of all chaos was created," whereupon the boy interrupted to ask "out of what chaos was created." The teacher lost his temper, said it was no business of his to know the answer, and told him to go to the philosophers. "Well," said Epicurus in effect, "that is what I shall do."

Additional interest attaches to the incident because in the mature philosophy of Epicurus the existence of chaos was denied. According to him the universe was eternal and had always been an orderly cosmos; all stories of divine creation were myths. In due time his disciples were to make fun of the Book of Genesis.

At the age of eighteen Epicurus was summoned to perform the required two years of military training in Athens, and the call chanced to coincide with the news of the untimely death of Alexander in 323 B.C. A rash war was immediately begun by the elated Athenians, which quickly ended in catastrophe; and so Epicurus became, as it were, an eyewitness of the last scene of the last act of the realistic drama that marked the transition from local democracy to world empire. The offending orators were executed by the Macedonians. This experience was not without its influence upon the youthful Epicurus, who subsequently condemned the political career and the whole program of education that prepared for it. His nonpolitical philosophy flourished in advance of nonpolitical Christianity.

This condemnation of the higher education placed Epicurus in the same position as St. Paul at Ephesus in later days, when he threatened the emolument of the silversmiths; vested interests were at stake. The rhetoricians, who depended upon students' fees, retorted madly by denouncing him as a dullard, an ignoramus, and an enemy of all culture.

These slanders continued to flourish throughout ancient times and are still repeated and believed by acquiescent modern scholars but refutation is not difficult. In reality Epicurus was an acute reasoner and in his youth he had made the round of the schools then flourishing.

Before his cadetship he was enrolled in Samos with Pamphilus the Platonist, probably for the usual four years, from the age of fourteen to eighteen. After his cadetship he studied with a capable Peripatetic, Praxiphanes of Rhodes, who was more interested in good writing than in oratorical rhetoric. Third and last on the list of able teachers was Nausiphanes of Teos, a shrewd and learned, though indolent, man, who perpetuated the teachings of Democritus, the atomist.

From this teacher Nausiphanes Epicurus parted in consequence of a violent quarrel, and it is probable that he had bickered with the previous two. He afterward denied all debt to any of them and boasted of being "self-taught." This boast bears a singular resemblance to the declaration of Paul to the Galatians: "But I certify you, brethren, that the gospel that was preached of me is not after man; for I neither received it of man, neither was I taught it."

The comparison ends itself abruptly, however, because Epicurus did not claim divine inspiration. He regarded himself as the originator of truth and his disciples so esteemed him. In his writings he never quoted authorities; his utterances were offered as oracles. He referred to his doctrines as "true philosophy" and his disciples lauded him as a god and the sole discoverer of truth. After the savior sentiment became popular they also spoke of him as a savior.

The consciousness of a mission to bring happiness to mankind seems to have come to him while studying with Nausiphanes. At any rate he gave up all hope of arriving at wisdom by the help of teachers and resumed his residence with his parents and three brothers at Colophon. This was a small but ancient city a few miles north of Ephesus and deserves to be regarded with some distinction. It was there during the ensuing years that Epicurus worked out his system of thought to completion. This was the only world philosophy and the only missionary philosophy produced by the Greeks and was destined to flourish openly for seven centuries, three before Christ and four afterward. Even in modern times its influence operates anonymously.

## Personality

In preparation for a brief recital of the doctrines of Epicurus certain paradoxical facts should be brought to attention and stored in mind. Of all Greek philosophers Epicurus is the only one who in point of appearance and demeanor would suggest the person of Christ. His bearded face, which is well known from surviving portrait busts, exhibits a quiet dignity and serenity of mien so suggestive of the popular concept of the countenance of Jesus as to be frequently remarked by the most disinterested observers. In ancient times this kindly face was universally known because of statues in public places and not less because of likenesses set into the finger rings of his followers. In Paul's own lifetime the reverence with which it was regarded provoked the scorn of the elder Pliny in Rome and at a later time the disgust of the churchman Origen in the East.

In harmony with this portraiture is the estimation of his personality as handed down in the tradition of his own school: "A truly sacred character and divinely gifted, the only man who has arrived at a knowledge of the true and the beautiful and has transmitted this knowledge to others, and the only man who has brought freedom to his followers."

In harmony with both portraiture and personality is the plan of life he recommended, a simple, unambitious way of living, far from the ignoble quest of wealth, power, and fame, characterized by courtesy combined with absolute veracity, good will to mankind, considerateness, loyalty to friends, benevolence, gratitude for past blessings, hope for the future, and in time of trouble patience.

Yet this threefold harmony of portraiture, personality, and attitudes — an historical preview of our conception of the appearance, character, and teachings of Jesus — must prompt us chiefly to realize the embarrassing predicament of Paul. The basis of reasoning upon which this plan of life was constructed could only be to him as horrifying as the practical precepts of the life were attractive. The plan was made to depend upon emancipation from the yoke of religion and the fear of death and divine wrath.

Yet this opposition of doctrine was only one aspect of the historical paradox. The more momentous aspect of it lay in the fact that the whole coherent structure of Epicurean materialism had been built up and solidified and disseminated over the Mediterranean world during the three centuries before the birth of Christ. It was consequently a necessity for Jesus and Paul to build up a substitute structure of thought in opposition to a system firmly and widely established and amply equipped in advance to oppose it and to criticize it.

All the armament of Epicurean logic which had been developed to combat Greek paganism and Platonic idealism was available from the outset for the crusade against the nascent Christianity. This conflict fell chiefly upon Paul, because it was his lot to carry the new gospel to the Greeks. For him the specific task was to build up a new structure of spirituality in the face of an entrenched and confident structure of materialism. It was the logic of the cross against the logic of the atom, an early phase of the long strife between science and religion. Epicurus himself became a sort of Antichrist.

## Peace and Safety

Epicurus, like Jesus, began his ministry, if one may so write, about the age of thirty, and it may be added that he exhibited an aggressiveness comparable to that of Jesus in cleansing the temple. For his first venture as a public teacher his choice fell upon Mytilene, a thriving city on the island of Lesbos. There he quickly exasperated the local philosophers, who were Platonists, by denouncing their whole program of education, and especially rhetoric, which was in high demand as preparing young men for a public career and for this reason jealously guarded as the money-making branch of the curriculum.

These enemies retaliated by accusing Epicurus of impiety, which was treason under Greek law and punishable by death; they prodded the civil authorities into action and incited the rabble against him. So vicious became the threat to his life that the sole way of escape was flight by ship in wintry seas.

By good luck he arrived safely at the refuge of his choice, the city of Lampsacus on the Hellespont, now the Dardanelles; but on the way he was in danger of death by exposure or of capture by pirates, and he narrowly escaped shipwreck. This painful experience was taken to heart. Never again did he invite persecution.

Instead he took the determination to confine himself to peaceful methods and even prescribed rules of safety for his followers in his Authorized Doctrines. Thus the words Peace and Safety became catchwords of his sect and unless we are aware of this fact we shall fail to recognize the meaning of Paul in First Thessalonians 5:3: "For when they shall say Peace and Safety, then sudden destruction cometh upon them." This version, however, leaves something to be desired; it would be more accurate to read: "For at the very time that the words Peace and Safety are on their lips, sudden destruction is hanging over them."

7

In Lampsacus, although destitute and a refugee, Epicurus received protection and speedily made powerful friends among the officials of the local court, and in particular won the friendship of one Idomeneus, a scholarly and affluent man, who continued to furnish him generous financial support throughout the rest of his long life. It was there also that he gathered about him a group of able disciples, especially three: Hermarchus, who had followed him from Mytilene, and Metrodorus and Polyaenus.

These men were to him what Timothy, Titus, and Luke were to Paul at a later time. Moreover, just as Paul numbered women among his workers, such as Priscilla, so Epicurus had one Themista, a talented woman of Lampsacus, who wrote a book long famous on the Vanity of Glory. This may have been in the hands of Ecclesiastes when he wrote, "Vanity of vanities, all is vanity," and it is certain that Cicero mentioned it in a speech before the Roman senate.

After four years of happy residence in Lampsacus Epicurus was advised to leave it for the same reason that had brought him there in the beginning, considerations of safety; war seemed to be imminent between the Macedonian kings of Asia. His choice fell upon Athens, the best location for the dissemination of a new philosophy.

Even there, however, he did not dare to offer himself as a public teacher. Such a venture would have brought him under the jurisdiction of the superintendent of education, known as the gymnasiarch, and the spirit of persecution was then abroad. Only the year before his arrival, which occurred in 306 B.C., a law had been passed imposing the penalty of death for any philosopher who should offer himself as a public teacher without a license from the governing bodies. The law was repealed within the year but Epicurus was taking no chances; he confined his instruction to his own house within the city walls and to a garden outside.

It was no part of his plan to educate the Athenians. Already he had staked his claims in larger spheres of influence. His biographer writes that "friends came from all parts and shared the life with him in the Garden," this being the name by which the school became popularly known. From the outset it was planned that every alumnus should become a missionary. The method was essentially "each one teach one." All were supplied with textbooks specially written for home study and group instruction.

The bond of union among members of the sect in all parts was friendship. They called themselves "Friends of Epicurus." It was for this reason that Paul sedulously avoids the words *friend* and *friendship*; they occur nowhere in his writings, although not infrequent elsewhere in the New Testament.

## Doctrines

While recognizing Epicurus as a venturesome innovator in ethics and education we must also bear in mind that no thinker, however rebellious, can escape the succession of thinkers and the tradition of culture into which he was born. Each individual is bound to adopt as much as he rejects. Epicurus, for instance, rejected the study of geometry as having no bearing on the practical life but he discerned the merit of the textbook style of writing that was perfected in that field by his contemporary Euclid. He recognized this unadorned way of writing as being specially adapted for the instruction of the multitudes whom he aspired to win over to his version of the happy life. He knew how to write artfully and was inclined toward the poetical, but he suppressed both of these tendencies in the interest of clarity, which he declared to be the sole requisite of style.

In pursuing this course he performed an unwitting service to Christianity by habituating the ancient public to the practice of reading plainly written textbooks on ethical subjects. He prepared the ground for Paul, in particular, who, like himself, felt the need of keeping in check the tendencies toward the rhetorical and the poetical.

In his textbooks Epicurus embodied the most neat and orderly system of knowledge ever put together in ancient times. It consisted of three parts, Canon, Physics, and Ethics, all of them known to Paul, as is revealed by specific references, if only we have learned to recognize the clues. Paul revealed his knowledge of the Canon by setting up a canon of his own; he recognized the Physics by postulating a different source of truth. He recognized the Ethics by adopting many of its teachings, changing the motivation.

By the canon was meant the criteria by which the truth was to be tested. These criteria or tests were three in number: Sensations, Feelings, and Anticipations, all of them furnished by Nature herself. To Epicurus Nature was the supreme teacher and Paul betrays his knowledge of this fact in First Corinthians 11:14 by writing: "Does not

Nature herself teach you?" It also comes quite naturally to him to write "according to nature" and "contrary to nature." The more significance attaches to this because nowhere in the New Testament does the word *nature* occur except in the Epistles of Paul himself and those of Peter and James.

That the Canon of Epicurus was known to Paul is demonstrated by First Corinthians 2, where he lucidly sets up his substitute, which is spiritual insight, not an endowment of Nature, but the gift of God. As for the Physics, Epicurus deduced from this his whole system of ethics and Paul reveals both his awareness of this and his reaction to it by the vehemence with which he insists that "all the treasures of wisdom and knowledge" are hidden in God. A positive assertion of this kind presumes a negative and this negative is assuredly Epicurean. Epicurus had virtually taught that all the treasures of wisdom and knowledge are hidden in Nature.

The Sensations are five, corresponding to the five senses. According to Epicurus these are man's direct contact with physical realities. He thinks of the mind as an automatic mechanism for processing the data of the senses and points out what a marvellous job they do of taking care of us on our daily rounds and keeping us from tripping over sleeping dogs or falling into ditches. He never claims infallibility for the sensations, as modern scholars wrongly assert. Only immediate sensations are to be trusted. For example, if the observer sees a man face to face he can be sure whether it is Plato; at the distance of half a mile he cannot be sure whether it is Plato or Aristotle. Only the face-to-face recognition is sure.

Paul's reaction to this is highly interesting; he rejects it in theory and adopts it in practice. For example, he employs the terminology of sensation in one of his finest verses, First Corinthians 13:12: "For now we see in a mirror, indistinctly, but then face to face." On the contrary, in Colossians 2:18 he pours scorn on the unnamed Epicurean, "taking his stand on what he has seen, puffed up without justification by the mind of the flesh" (the translation is our own). Much of importance awaits to be said on this topic in Chapter IX.

The Feelings are two, pleasure and pain, Nature's educators, her Go and Stop signals, by which she trains man and beast to recognize what is good for him and what is evil in his environment. As criteria of truth the Feelings operate on both physical and social levels of life.

For example, justice gives pleasure and injustice hurts no less than a blow or a burn.

What is meant by an Anticipation or, as Epicurus calls it, a Prolepsis, is not difficult to explain, though generally misunderstood. Epicurus believed that man is preconditioned by Nature for living in his physical and social environment. On the physical level he is equipped in advance by Sensations and Feelings. On the level of social and intellectual life he is equipped with innate ideas, such as that of justice, which exist in advance of experience and so anticipate experience, being for that reason called Anticipations.

He thought of the mentality of the grown man as being anticipated in the newborn infant just as the whole physical body is anticipated in the embryo before birth. He even insisted that man is born with an innate notion of the divine nature, but only as "blissful and incorruptible," not wrathful. In spite of this fact his usual reputation was that of an atheist.

## Physics

Under the term *physics* the Greeks included all natural science, the division into various branches such as chemistry and biology being destined to await the modern era. Epicurus chose to sponsor the atomic theory of the constitution of matter, whether animal or mineral. The term *atom* signified the minimum self-existing particle of matter. The word itself means "indivisible" and in order to express this idea in Latin the Romans coined the word *individuus*, from which we have the word "individual."

The whole theory of physics was reduced by Epicurus to Twelve Elementary Principles and a syllabus bearing this title was published for the use of his disciples. This list of Principles, it may be interposed, was the most lucid and orderly ever drawn up in ancient times, and with one exception would have been received with respect down to the date of an event so recent as the fission of the atom. By way of illustration the first seven are here listed with some adaptation to modern terminology:

1. Matter is uncreatable.
2. Matter is indestructible.
3. The universe consists of atoms and space.
4. All existing things are either atoms or compounds of atoms.

5. The atoms are infinite in multitude.
6. Space is infinite in extent.
7. The atoms are always in action.

As was bound to happen, this whole system became known to the enemies of Epicurus by that particular Principle which was most offensive and provocative of ridicule, the third. This was offensive because it implied that the soul of man itself was composed of atoms, just as the body itself, and therefore subject to dissolution, just as the body. It was especially open to ridicule because the atoms were such insignificant things upon which to base a whole system of knowledge. In Galatians 4:9 Paul sneered at them as "the weak and beggarly elements."

For the reason that the atom was the smallest thing imaginable the word was also used of time and in First Corinthians 15:52 it is translated "in a moment" and this is amplified as "in the twinkling of an eye," referring to the miracle of the general resurrection. This is the sole occurrence of the word in the Bible.

For the reason that all existing things were thought to be made of atoms, just as all words are made of letters, it was usual also to denote the atoms by the word *elements*, which properly means letters of the alphabet. The etymology of this word *elements* is curious and enlightening. The names of the letters seem to have come to us through the Romans from the Etruscans, who for some reason began with L M N, that is, el em en, hence Latin *elementa*, instead of beginning with A B C.

Under the name of elements the atoms are mentioned six times in the New Testament, three times simply as elements and three times as "elements of the universe," an unmistakable recognition of the third Elementary Principle of Epicurus: "The universe consists of atoms and space." In the light of the fact that Epicurus asserted the atoms to be indestructible it is especially interesting to read the defiant prediction in Second Peter 3:10 and 12: "the elements will be dissolved with fire" and "the elements will melt with fire."

The translators of 1611 were quite at a loss in interpreting these verses and the authors of the Revised Standard, not suspecting the influence of Epicurus, resorted to a farfetched explanation based upon belief in tutelary spirits of the universe; but there is no real justification for inserting the word *spirits*, as in Colossians 2:8 and 20, "the elemental spirits of the universe."

## The Universe

As for the universe itself, Epicurus asserted in various writings, including his list of Elementary Principles, that it was infinite in extent. On this assumption, he was bound to believe also in an infinite number of worlds, more or less like our own earth; if there were only one world, the universe would not be infinite. Paul, of course, believed in a finite universe, consisting of heaven and earth, which God had created and would also destroy and rebuild. This idea of divine creation was, of course, ridiculed by Epicurus; he declared that "the universe was the same as it always had been and always would be the same," and this very declaration is placed in the mouths of "scoffers," though not precisely quoted, in Second Peter 3:4.

A curious detail is worthy of mention here. According to Epicurus, the one thing that never changed was the atom; it was eternal. However, the word he employs for "eternal" is not the word used repeatedly in the New Testament in this sense; but when Paul in Romans 1:20 writes of "the eternal power" of God, it is the uncommon word of Epicurus that he employs, which occurs elsewhere only in a similar context in Jude 6. It might seem as if Paul were gently twitting the Epicurean reader of his day. He certainly exhibits a familiarity with the Epicurean vocabulary which will not bear our neglect.

To return to our topic, the universe: in spite of divergence of opinion on the point of its extent, there was one detail in respect of which Epicurus and Paul agreed to differ with their respective races and agree with one another, the abolition of Hell. The Greeks knew this institution under the name of Acheron or Hades, the Jews as Gehenna or Sheoul. Both races thought of the world as divided into three regions: one above, one below, and another in between. Both Epicurus and Paul recognized but two regions, though for different reasons.

According to Epicurus the gods were incapable of wrath and consequently indifferent toward wickedness. According to Paul, God was capable of wrath but deliberately turned his back upon the wicked and abandoned them to their sins unless they chose to recognize the resurrected Christ. They were not punished but doomed to instant annihilation on the last day; "the wages of sin is death." Of temporal punishment there was none and consequently no need of Hell.

Just as Epicurus and Paul were in unison in abolishing a realm of punishment, so they were agreed upon regarding the resultant universe as two regions, the earthly and the heavenly. Yet there is a sharp limit to this agreement. It was the teaching of Epicurus that the abode of the gods was located in the spaces between the worlds, regions of peace and perpetual light. This coincides fairly well, of course, with Paul's conception of heaven; but the subsidiary teaching of Epicurus that these gods were totally indifferent to human wickedness was abhorrent.

His vehement reaction to this shocking doctrine may be found in Ephesians 6:12, where we read in the Revised Standard of "the spiritual hosts of wickedness in the heavenly places." A more detailed interpretation of this verse, however, must await its turn in Chapter VI.

## Ethics

Of the ethics of Epicurus it may be said that in antiquity no other design for living was judged to be more alluring. His teachings were compared to the voices of the Sirens, those mythical maidens whose sweetness of voice was said to cast an irresistible spell. In the Rome of Cicero's day the foremost teacher of the creed was given the name of Siro, that is, the man who lured men like a Siren.

The testimony of the illustrious churchman St. Augustine confirms the judgment of the pagans; he characterized the creed by three alluring words: Pleasure, Suavity, and Peace.

The word *pleasure* was merely an unfortunate choice of terms for happiness. The truth of this statement is made clear by a saying of Epicurus himself: "Even on the rack the wise man is happy." Under torture the wise man could not affirm that he was enjoying pleasure; but, like the Christian martyr of later times, he could still lay claim to happiness. The pleasure of Epicurus was not the pleasure of the flesh, though his enemies willfully chose to thus misconstrue it.

Happiness in his view of things consisted in the memory of pleasures past, the enjoyment of pleasures present, and the hope of pleasures to come. This teaching was summed up in a famous saying: "Pleasure is the beginning and the end of the happy life."

Plato had committed himself to the doctrine that continuous pleasure was impossible. Epicurus wrote to one of his young disciples: "It is to continuous pleasures that I invite you." This invitation was matched by Paul, who wrote in Philippians 4:4: "Rejoice in the Lord always; again I will say, Rejoice."

14

Fullness was elevated to the rank of an alluring word in the language of Epicurus. In order to reconcile mankind to the surrender of belief in immortality he argued that fullness of pleasure could be attained in this mortal life, because the list of pleasures is limited and all natural desires for pleasure can be satisfied. With pleasure, of course, Paul could have no commerce and he studiously avoids the very name of it, but the idea of fullness was alluring, and so, in the compass of a single Epistle, that to the Ephesians, we find mention of "the fullness of him who fills all in all," "the fullness of God," and "the measure of the stature of the fullness of Christ."

The blessed idea of fullness as a goal and consummation of living has been retained but the content of meaning has been utterly transformed; the word has been lifted bodily out of one context of thought and incorporated into another.

Freedom is bound to be an attractive word in all ages. Epicurus held out this lure to the world of his day. By him it was defined as freedom from fears: from fear of fate, fear of the calamities of life, fear of vengeful gods, of death, and punishment after death. Christianity was bound to have an offer to substitute for this; and Paul writes in Galatians 5:13: "For it was on the presumption of freedom that you Galatians were called, brethren," and to this he adds, with silent reference to Epicurus: "only not to the kind of freedom that means license to the flesh." The new freedom is emancipation from the bondage of sin.

## Faith, Hope, and Love

The discovery of faith as a virtue was an incident in the life story of Epicurus. One of the thinkers who captured his interest in his student days was Pyrrho, the skeptic, who had resigned himself to belief in the impossibility of certainty in knowledge. Epicurus, however, was not the man to resign himself; he rebelled, discerning that uncertainty was incompatible with assured peace of mind. So he became a dogmatist, the first dogmatist among the Greek philosophers.

He gave up controversy and began to write as one having authority. Among other writings, for example, he published his forty Authorized Doctrines, veritable Articles of Faith, which his disciples were to commit to memory. Thus faith made its first appearance as faith in doctrine. The solid core of truth in this teaching was too precious to be cast overboard by his successors. Among these was Paul, who discerned even a higher value in the new virtue and transformed its meaning to denote faith in the resurrected Christ, though in its more general aspect it became faith in God.

The virtue of hope has a similar history. It was Epicurus who first assigned to it a specific role in a plan of life. Paul found for it a new role in the plan of salvation. Epicurus deemed it necessary in planning the mortal life to make a rational choice of attitudes; hope was the rational attitude to assume toward the future; the wise man should so order his life as to be justified in the hope of pleasures to come. This function of hope was recognized by Paul when he wrote, "Love hopeth all things," but a new and specific meaning for the word was found in the hope of the resurrection.

Love, like hope, had one aspect for Epicurus and two for Paul. To his followers Epicurus offered the lure of friendship and good companionship; in their own circles his disciples were known as "Friends of Epicurus." Paul never employs the words *friend* or *friendship*; he brushes them aside and substitutes the larger concept of the love of God. His readers are urgently exhorted to love one another but this brotherly love becomes a particular aspect of the larger concept, the love of God. To love one another is to imitate God.

The fact remains, nevertheless, that the philosophy of friendship flourished in advance of the religion of love and created a climate of feeling favorable to its reception.

These three topics will be suitably amplified in the chapter on Faith, Hope, and Love.

## Suavity and Peace

Of the three watchwords of the Epicureans cited by St. Augustine, pleasure, suavity, and peace, the first has been discussed above. Suavity and peace await brief mention.

Suavity was defined by Cicero, not without having the Epicureans in mind, as "an agreeableness of speech and manners." This virtue defined the proper attitude to assume toward all men and especially toward outsiders, just as Paul advises in Colossians 4:5–6, as the Revised Standard renders it: "Conduct yourselves wisely toward outsiders, making the most of the time. Let your speech always be gracious." Within the Epicurean circle this suavity or courtesy was to be joined with candor. Friends were to correct one another without animus and accept correction without resentment, just as Paul writes in Ephesians 4:15 under the formula, "speaking the truth in love." This topic will be touched upon here and there in the chapters that follow.

Just as Epicurus held out to mankind the pleasures of friendship and good companionship, seasoned with courtesy and candor, so he offered the enjoyment of peace. Peace presents two aspects. So far as it means peace of mind, it overlaps the concept of freedom, which among other things means freedom from fears. This has been dealt with already.

So far as peace of mind means happy relationships in the family and community, this depends chiefly upon the virtue of considerateness, of which Epicurus made a specialty. While this virtue applies to all contacts of the individual with others, a single particular may be cited for illustration.

It was the custom of the ancients to beat their slaves, often without mercy. That Epicurus was opposed to this corporal punishment we are informed by his biographer; and Paul, when listing the qualifications of a good bishop in First Timothy 3:3, warns specifically that he must not be "given to blows but considerate," employing the Epicurean word for considerate, which nowhere occurs in the Gospels. In this passage no ancient reader would have failed to observe that the reference is to the treatment of slaves; even their feelings deserved consideration if family life was to be peaceful.

Thus the philosophy of peace was flourishing in advance of the religion of peace. What Paul did was to rehabilitate the whole concept of peace and assemble all aspects of it under a single phrase, "the peace of God." It may be added that the phrases "gospel of peace" and "God of peace" are peculiar to his Epistles.

## Plausible Reasonings

In his Epistle to the Colossians, 2:4, Paul issues a warning against the "enticing words" or "beguiling speech" of the Epicurean competitors, whom he will never name. These translations are imprecise; the meaning is rather "plausible reasonings," and we shall improve our understanding if we succeed in pinning the meaning down to specific references.

What Paul fears is the attractiveness of the doctrines compiled by Epicurus in numerous textbooks. These doctrines were simply stated and in forms that were readily memorized. As a specimen we may choose the classification of the desires, which was widely known in antiquity: "Of the desires some are natural and necessary; some are natural but not necessary; and others are neither natural nor necessary." This is Authorized Doctrine 29.

The neatness of this classification was acknowledged even by Cicero. It is not only neat and easy to remember; it is also easy to expand. The natural and necessary desires are four: for food, drink, clothing, and housing. Jesus himself may have had this list in mind when, as recorded in Matthew 6:25, he said, "what ye shall eat or what ye shall drink; nor yet for your body, what ye shall put on."

The point that is regularly urged by Epicurus is this, that it wounds our vanity "but occasions no pain to the body if we lack the garment resplendent with purple and adorned with striking designs in thread of gold, providing only we have a plain cloak to fend off the cold." To covet costly raiment is to labor under a delusion, the false idea that it contributes to happiness.

The second class of desires, those that are natural but not necessary, are sexual, as also those for luxurious viands and rare wines. No harm results if these are not gratified.

The third class, the desires that are neither natural nor necessary, is curiously defined in an ancient commentary as referring to "crowns and statues in public places." Greek statesmen were sometimes awarded circlets of gold as rewards for public service. The warning of Epicurus in this instance is against all highly competitive careers, which bring no real happiness. Paul too has warnings to issue against the competitive spirit; in Philippians 1:17 he even identifies men who, thinking to cause him affliction, "proclaim the gospel of Christ out of a spirit of competition."

If now we make a last scrutiny of this classification, we should observe that its popularity made of the desires a foremost topic in the public mind. Epicurus, of course, recognized many desires as natural and only potentially injurious. This attitude was untenable for Paul. In his view of things, the very name of *desire* was in the same class as the word *pleasure*, both of them tainted with suspicion because of the association with the flesh. Thus the word *pleasure* is banned from his vocabulary and the word *desire* used regularly in an evil sense.

This very cautiousness of Paul, however, reveals both his fears and his awareness of the Epicurean teaching. This awareness is revealed to

18

us sometimes by a single word. For instance, in a certain saying Epicurus employs the phrase, "injurious desires," which is found also in First Timothy 6:9, though even this adjective *injurious* occurs nowhere else in the New Testament. When Paul recognizes "injurious desires," he tacitly recognizes desires that are not injurious, just as Epicurus taught.

The evidence is not confined, however, to one word. Paul also employs a word that was probably coined by Epicurus, *kenodoxia,* as in Philippians 2:3, where mistranslations are the rule. The reasoning behind this is simple; if we allow our desires to make our decisions for us, we become victims of a delusion or cherish an illusion. For example, we imagine that riches spell happiness.

About the topic of wealth and poverty and "the deceitfulness of riches" Epicurus had much to say himself and regarded it as of such importance as to turn it over to his trusted colleague Metrodorus for amplification in a separate treatise. Opposed to the delusive vision of happiness that went with wealth was the genuine happiness that resulted from contentment with little, and much remains to be said about this in connection with Philippians 4:10–13 and First Timothy 6:6–10.

In the meantime, we may quote four aphorisms of the sort that justify the popularity of Epicurean teachings in the times of the New Testament:

Nothing is enough for a man for whom enough is too little.

Of contentment with little the greatest fruit is freedom.

To acquire great wealth and live a life of freedom is impossible.

It were better for you to recline upon a cheap cot in peace of mind than to have a gilded bedstead and a luxurious table and a soul in turmoil.

## Theology

The jaundiced tradition that denounces Epicurus as an atheist is sheer slander. In point of fact he regarded himself as a religious reformer, who was recalling mankind to a more pure and lofty conception of the divine being.

He maintained the belief in the existence of gods to be innate in the mind of man and to exist there in advance of all religious experience. As evidence of this he cited the universal response of mankind to the belief in the existence of gods.

19

He conceived of the divine nature as "blessed and incorruptible." Upon his disciples he urged the necessity of associating no idea with the divine nature that was inconsistent with this perfection of happiness and incorruptibility. The supreme duty of man was reverence; the very names of the gods should be sacred. No task was to be ascribed to them that was by its nature onerous, such as superintending the operations of the universe, which was to be thought self-operating under natural laws.

The very first of his Authorized Doctrines declared the gods to be incapable of anger. Anger was a disturbing emotion and a symptom of weakness; to ascribe such an emotion to the gods was to detract from their sanctity and to diminish their claim to the worship of mankind. Upon this worship as embodied in the public festivals, especially the music, he placed supreme importance and among his sayings is one to the effect that "the wise man will derive more enjoyment than other men from the state festivals."

If this elimination of anger from celestial minds was offensive to orthodox pagan Greeks, it was still more so when it became known to orthodox Jews, whose Jehovah bore a unique reputation as a God of wrath. Equally offensive was the removal of the gods from all participation in human affairs, which involved the rejection of belief in divine prophecy, in miracles, and divine providence.

These teachings were judged to cancel all the merit that resided in the demand of Epicurus for more reverence for godhead; they relegated him to the evil eminence of being the archenemy of religion and a sort of Antichrist.

We should recall, however, the words of Paul in Second Thessalonians 2:3: "for that day will not come, unless the rebellion comes first." In the procession of time the rebellion of Epicurus did come first and as a consequence the God of wrath of the Old Testament was transformed into the God of love of the New Testament.

# PHILIPPIANS

## Their God Is the Belly

THE Epistle to the Philippians happens to be suitable for beginning a study of Epicureanism in the writings of Paul. The two parties in each community from which the chief opposition arose to the invading Christianity are here typically but briefly presented. The first was the fundamentalist party among the Jews, which is unmistakably identified even for the modern reader by the word *circumcision*. The second party consisted of the ubiquitous and numerous disciples of Epicurus, of which the identity was as plainly manifest to the ancient reader as was that of the Jewish fundamentalists, though to the modern reader the symbols of identification have long since become meaningless.

In order to restore meaning to these symbols the reader must learn first where to expect them and in order to know where to expect them he must know how Paul's letters are put together. They are composed according to a good Greek formula, which was recognized and recommended by Aristotle. If from each Epistle the salutation and concluding messages be lopped off, the body of the letter will be seen to consist of three parts, a beginning, middle, and end.

The beginning is conciliatory: Paul compliments the community for its faith or for its kindness to him in the past. This is the bid for good will and a sympathetic hearing, well known to rhetoricians as the *captatio benevolentiae*. The middle part contains warnings, expositions of doctrine, and scoldings, if any, which might possibly try the good will and patience of readers. The concluding passage is reserved for friendly admonition and exhortation.

This happens to be a good Epicurean pattern. The same formula is employed by the Epicurean poet Lucretius. He begins each book with a flourish of enthusiasm, packs all the prosaic material in the middle, and takes care to conclude, as if leaving the lectern and mounting the pulpit, with a lofty discourse upon ethics. Even the three extant letters of Epicurus conclude with brief moral exhortation.

It is in the middle part of the Epistles of Paul that offensive doctrines of the Epicureans are to be expected; it is in the last section of each Epistle that adoptable features of the friendly Epicurean ethics are to be expected. Of the two kinds of doctrine, the offensive and the adoptable, the former are the easier to identify. For example, in the Epistle to the Philippians we should have but little trouble in learning to identify the Epicureans either by the words "their god is the belly" or "they glory in their shame." On the other hand, a keener discernment must be acquired to recognize Epicurean teaching toward the end in 4:11: "for I have learned in whatever state I am, therewith to be content."

When once we have become thoroughly alerted to the implications of Paul's words and phrases the references to the Epicureans will prove to be numerous. For example, when he speaks in 3:18 of "the enemies of the cross of Christ," this denotation of the rival sect will be found elaborated in First Corinthians, where the logic of the Epicureans is opposed to "the word of the cross," that is, spirituality. Again, when he writes in 3:19, "Their end is destruction," this doom is specifically predicted for the Epicureans in First Thessalonians 5:3, where they are identified by their catchwords Peace and Safety. Again, when in 3:19 he writes, "with minds set on earthly things," the antithesis between "things that are on earth" and "things that are above," with demonstrable reference to Epicureanism, may be found elaborated in Colossians 3.

## Their God Is the Belly

All of these allusions are damning enough but the more serious are two (3:19): "their god is the belly" and "they glory in their shame." Both reproaches are as old as Epicureanism itself. The former has been the longer lived; it may be found in any English dictionary today by looking up the word *epicure*, which will be found to denote a sensualist and especially one who is given over to the pleasures of the stomach. In the Middle Ages the idea was expressed in pictures. In one of these

Epicurus is represented in company with Sardanapalus, an infamous oriental voluptuary.

It mattered little that this charge was false. It has been rightly said that Epicurus is the most calumniated of all philosophers. His offense, in the eyes of his enemies, was to have reached the conclusion that pleasure was the chief good in life or, to be more precise, the chief end of man as demonstrated by the teaching of Nature herself. Even the newly born, Epicurus pointed out, whether brute or human, reaches out for pleasure as the greatest good and shrinks from pain as the greatest evil.

In the judgment of his enemies, it was not to be chalked up to his credit that by the teaching of the very same Nature who identified pleasure as the greatest good the definition of true pleasure was so narrowed as to demand of her devotees a strictness of life that was almost ascetic. The pleasure of drinking, for example, was to be limited by the quenching of thirst; the pleasure of eating was to be limited by the satisfaction of hunger.

Of these principles Paul was fully aware, as he was of the whole doctrine of Epicurus, and in Colossians 2:23, he even shows himself compelled to concede some merit in them, although to ascertain his exact attitude the translation will require correction. This will be one of the many passages where the knowledge of Epicurean doctrine will help us to discover what Paul was intending to say.

In addition to the general sponsorship of pleasure there were specific teachings that lent plausibility to the charge that "their god is the belly." One of these stems from Metrodorus, able lieutenant of Epicurus: "The pleasure of the stomach is the beginning and the root of all good, and in this the things of wisdom and the refinements of life have their standard of reference."

Quoted out of context this judgment exhibits a shocking rawness. It must be appraised, however, as part of a genetic approach to the study of ethics. It presumes that human life develops by stages: infancy, childhood, adolescence, and maturity. The pleasure of the stomach is the first one known in infancy; other organs with their respective pleasures come to activity one by one. The mind matures last of all and must be regarded as an organ of the physical being no less than the stomach. The poet Lucretius, for example, chooses to insist upon the point that the mind is an organ of the body no less than the ear.

This adds up to the conclusion that pleasure is a common denominator of all bodily activity, mental activity not excluded, and justifies the declaration quoted above that "in this . . . the refinements of life have their standard of reference." The timorous thinker would rather embrace unreason than be escorted by reason to such a verdict.

Epicurus, however, was quite immune to the timidity of the conventional moralist with regard to pleasure. He maintained that pleasure and health go together just as pain and disease; nor was it any more possible to dissociate pleasure from the healthy life than it was possible to dissociate heat from fire. Pleasure, he taught, is the ruling motive from the cradle to the grave. Even virtue is practiced for the sake of pleasure; the good life and the happy life go together just like sweetness and honey. He flouted the idea of Plato that the value of a virtue is diminished if accompanied by pleasure. "I spit upon the beautiful," he wrote, "if it fails to give pleasure."

## They Glory in Their Shame

It was the sponsorship of pleasure that from the first drew upon Epicurus the imputation of shamelessness. The very name of pleasure can be frightening to conventional morality and pious respectability. Aristotle ventured the judgment that even people who believed that pleasure had the sanction of Nature as the chief end of man would hesitate to sponsor the doctrine. Cicero, speaking for the man in public life, observed the impossibility of sponsoring pleasure "in the forum, in the senate, or in the camp."

Epicurus was denounced by Timon, a vulgar satirist, as "the lowest dog among the physicists," the dog being to the Greeks the symbol of shamelessness because it does in public what human beings veil with privacy. It is this satirical jab of the Greek Timon that enables us to interpret with unassailable certainty the reference to Epicureans in 3:2: "Beware of the dogs." It is this idea that Paul with his customary tenacity of topic is elaborating in 3:19: "they glory in their shame."

A variant of this general outcry was authored by the Platonists, who declared that to sponsor pleasure as the end of living was to bring life down to the level of the beasts. A censorious Stoic named Hierocles capped this chorus of denunciations by the acrid epigram: "To believe that pleasure is the end is the creed of a prostitute; to deny providence is beneath even a prostitute."

24

Incidentally, the popular opinion that the Stoics were the outspoken and courageous sect is questionable. Their outspokenness was rather an affectation and their real intention was to astonish rather than to defy. Essentially they were reactionaries, fundamentalists in revolt against Epicurean hedonism. They made a great show of sponsoring the words and concepts that salve the consciences and flatter the vanity of mankind: virtue, duty, divine providence, reason. The hypocrites rallied to their side. Meanwhile, it was around Epicurus and the memory of him that "all the dogs of philosophy were barking" — to borrow a phrase from the churchman Lactantius — Stoic dogs foremost among them.

It required no courage to preach that virtue is the chief good. It did require courage to declare that the practice of virtue cannot be separated from pleasure, that the gods were not superintending engineers of a complicated universe, and that the divine being was incapable of anger.

Even the Authorized Doctrines of Epicurus would have afforded ground for the accusation that "they gloried in their shame." In certain of these Doctrines the founder had stated his teachings on the subject of pleasure with a directness that seemed like shameless defiance of orthodox morality. One of them reads: "No pleasure is evil in itself but the practices productive of certain pleasures may result in distresses outweighing by many times the pleasures themselves." This means that all pleasures are good; the evil lies solely in their consequences.

In another of these doctrines he went so far as to assert that if the pleasures of profligates dispelled the fears of the mind and similar disturbing emotions, "we would never have cause to blame them, glutting themselves with pleasures from every side and experiencing no pain of body or distress of mind from any quarter, in which the evil lies."

This statement alone, originally published in the heat of controversy, even if no other evidence were citable, would justify the censure, "they glory in their shame."

## Minds Set on Earthly Things

The mention of "minds set on earthly things" is a further identification of Epicureans. This refers to the fact that Epicurus based his whole system of ethics, including a very definite design for living, upon his Physics, of which the basic doctrine declared: "The universe consists of atoms and void," implying definitely that nothing else really existed.

A more suitable place for amplifying this topic will be presented by the Epistle to the Galatians. Here it may be profitable, however, to prepare the way by an advance notice to the effect that this material-ism, based upon the atomic hypothesis, accounts in large part for a characteristic dualism in Paul's thought. The atoms stand for "earthly things," that is, "things that are on earth" as opposed to "things that are above," well known from Colossians 3:2. Another guise of the same dualism is discerned in the opposition between the flesh and the Spirit and in "the desires of the flesh" and "the desires of the Spirit," as also in "the works of the flesh" and "the works of the Spirit," long stamped on Christian minds by Galatians 5:16–25.

This dualism, a fruitful and fascinating feature of Pauline thought, was inherent in the philosophy of Epicurus, who thought of this earth we inhabit as a place "where the forces of destruction always prevail in the end over the forces of creation," and set in opposition to it the heavenly regions, "where the forces of preservation always prevail over the forces of destruction."

We shall find this distinction making its reappearance in our study of the illustrious fifteenth chapter of First Corinthians. It will be seen to be there typified by the Pauline expository invention of "the first Adam" and "the last Adam," the former the recipient at God's hand of mortal life — that is, corruption — the second, Jesus Christ, endowed by God with the power to bestow immortal spiritual life — that is, incorruption. This will be one of the many items of interpretation that serve to uncover for us the background of Paul's thought, just as a later painting is sometimes peeled off the wall of an ancient church to reveal a fresco of earlier Christianity.

Such discoveries may have for their reward an improved understand-ing and more precise translations.

## Rejoice in the Lord Always

In the last chapter of Philippians Paul turns to friendly admonitions, of which the firm but genial Epicurus had made a specialty long before him. It is in concluding sections of each letter that these adoptable teachings of the friendly pagan sect may most often be detected. A specimen may sometimes be identified in the simplest and most innocent admonition.

Take, for example, 3:1, "rejoice in the Lord," and 4:4, "Rejoice in the Lord always." Why should Paul say "always" and why should he seek emphasis by repetition, "Again I will say, Rejoice"? Behind this lies a chapter of discussion in the history of philosophy. Plato became rather notorious after his death for having put himself in a position to deny that a man could be happy all the time. He had associated pleasure with the various organs of the body. These, of course, cannot be in a state of excitement all the time. Consequently there must be peaks of pleasure separated by intervals devoid of pleasure or by "mixed states," in which pain and pleasure are simultaneously present.

Epicurus, who followed closely upon Plato in point of time, vigorously rejected the assumption that continuous happiness was impossible. "If your analysis of pleasure leads to this conclusion," he said in effect, "then your analysis of pleasure is wrong." His solution was to associate pleasure with health just as pain is associated with disease. It follows that if a man can be healthy all the time, he can also be happy all the time.

Moreover, he denied that pleasure and pain could be mixed, as Plato claimed. He maintained instead that pain could be subtracted from pleasure, leaving a balance of pleasure, and that this was true in all but the most acute illnesses. Hence Epicurus is on record as writing to a youthful correspondent: "As for myself, it is to continuous pleasures that I invite you." His aim is to immunize the minds of his disciples against Platonic teachings without naming the adversary, an example that Paul copied in his treatment of Epicurus.

If we now bear in mind, as we ought, that Paul is addressing himself to communities in which Epicureans are numerous and that he is willing to become "as a Greek to the Greeks" in order to bring some of them over to his creed, could he afford to offer them less happiness than Epicurus had offered? Hardly. Therefore, his "Rejoice in the Lord always" may be taken as a substitute for the words of his competitor, "It is to continuous pleasures that I invite you." Yet how completely the motivation has changed! In the logic of Epicurus pleasure is continuous because it can no more be separated from living than sweetness from honey; even the invalid can subtract the pain from the pleasure, leaving a balance of pleasure. The reason for the Christian's rejoicing, on the contrary, is the imminence of the second coming: "The Lord is at hand."

Incidentally, the recognition of this fact reveals an error of translation in the Revised Standard, which reads in 4:5: "Let all men know your forbearance." It is not forbearance that this happy expectation demands but consistency; unless they rejoice their conduct will not be in keeping with their belief. Consequently, for the sake of precision we should read: "Let your consistency be known to all men."

It may be interjected, by the way, that the Greek word here rendered "consistency" occurs only in the Epistles and is a favorite of the Epicureans. It denotes propriety in matters of conduct, that is, what befits or becomes a person in a particular case.

## Whatsoever Things Are True

Paul's reluctant partiality for the vocabulary of Epicurus often supplies the clue that leads to precision of interpretation, and, as already mentioned, this is especially true of the concluding sections of the Epistles, where adoptable items of the friendly creed most often present themselves. Take for an example the familiar verse 4:8, which begins, "Finally, brethren, whatsoever things are true, whatsoever things are honest."

As a devotional reading this euphonious passage has been casting its spell over innumerable congregations for the space of centuries, but how many of the worshipers who have experienced comfort and uplift from the sound of it could explain exactly what is meant by "whatsoever things are lovely"? Would the translators themselves be capable of explaining? To press this question might prove to be embarrassing.

In advance of the experiment of trying to discover what this verse would have signified to an Epicurean a word of caution is in order. It is not being denied that Paul was capable of using his language artfully, but it will be emphatically denied that he was ever willing to sacrifice meaning for the sake of euphony. It will be consistently assumed instead that his ideas are clean-cut and his references definite at all times. The problem will be to pinpoint the reference and to bring the meaning into focus.

In seeking help from Epicurus to explain Paul it deserves also to be brought to knowledge that this procedure involves a shocking rivalry of loyalties. In the Greek language the name *Epicurus* signifies "helper" or "succorer" and this may account in part for Paul's detestation of it and unwillingness to mention it. To concede to the adversary the title of helper, which by implication belonged to Jesus, was only one degree less repellent than to know that his disciples knew him as a savior, which they did. Epicurus became virtually a sort of Antichrist.

This understandable aversion is nevertheless not unmixed with reluctant admiration, which is also understandable, because Epicurus and his disciples had surpassed all others in their shrewd studies of human behavior. Paul's admiration is revealed in the words he employs.

It will be best for us to begin with "whatsoever things are lovely," because the word *lovely* is so very vague. There is no vagueness in its Greek counterpart, *prosphiles,* which applies to a person's demeanor and signifies "friendly" or "disposed to make friends." It is citable in Epicurean writings and in the New Testament only in this verse. The disciples of Epicurus were urged "all at the same time to wear a smile and practice their philosophy." They were a cheerful and ingratiating breed of men, aiming "to make friends with as many people as possible." They made a cult of friendliness.

It becomes manifest, therefore, that what Paul is urging upon the Philippians is to let their thoughts dwell upon "whatever makes for friendliness." The meaning is clean-cut.

Now that we have discovered Paul to be speaking of the proper demeanor for Christians we are in a better position to make a try for the meaning of "whatsoever things are of good report" or "whatever is gracious," as the Revised Standard has it. Both of these are needlessly vague. The Greek word here employed is the opposite of "blasphemous," which originally meant "slanderous." So Paul's meaning becomes clear; he is urging the Philippians to let their thoughts dwell upon "whatever makes for charity in speaking of others."

Next let attention be turned to "whatsoever things are honest" or, as in the Revised Standard, "whatever is honorable." The Greek word is *semnos* and means neither "honest" nor "honorable" but "worthy of reverence." It is used in the New Testament only by Paul and was a favorite of Epicurus. The latter demanded reverence for himself as the discoverer of truth and declared the principle: "Reverence for the wise man is a great blessing for him who feels the reverence." Moreover, he required of each disciple to show reverence for all who were farther advanced than himself on the way to wisdom.

Let us next scrutinize Paul's own use of this Epicurean word. In First Timothy 3:8 and 11 and Titus 2:2 he requires that deacons, elders, and women should so deport themselves "as to be worthy of reverence." Conversely, he is urging the Philippians always to display reverence toward those who had been appointed to positions of superiority over them, precisely as Epicurus had demanded reverence for those who were farther advanced in wisdom.

In other words, Paul is making the Christian pattern of behavior acceptable to Epicurean converts by adapting to the needs of the new community the very pattern of behavior to which they were already habituated. In his own words, he was making himself "as a Greek to the Greeks," which means "as an Epicurean to the Epicureans."

The requirements of precision will be served if we translate this as "whatever makes for reverence." The same exhortation expressed in other words may be found as a parting admonition in First Thessalonians 5:12 and Hebrews 13:7 and 17.

In dealing with the remaining items of Paul's list of injunctions the principle should still apply, that his reference is invariably precise. For example, in the case of "whatever is pure," the reference is to fornication and homosexual practices. It is a fact no less deplorable than well authenticated that these vices were often condoned by Greek philosophers, even by Plato, as Cicero conceded. It is not true, however, as sometimes asserted, that the Christians were the first to set their faces against such inchastities. Epicurus had taken the same stand three centuries before.

Plato had even dreamed that the passion of the flesh could be sublimated into a passion for knowledge and it was in reply to this astonishing teaching that Epicurus retorted crisply: "Sexual intercourse never did anyone any good and it is fortunate if it does no harm." He was unable to call it an offense against the gods, because he declared them indifferent to human wickedness, but he did denounce it for its ugly fruits, which he took pains to enumerate.

In this instance we may recognize yet another segment of the common ground of doctrine between Epicureanism and Christianity which eased the transition from the age of philosophy to that of religion. The truth of this statement is not canceled by the fact that the sponsorship of pleasure by Epicurus was sometimes made an excuse for loose living. Even Paul's doctrine of election by God for salvation was seized upon by some as a license to sin; if a man had been elected for salvation, it was argued, laxity of conduct could not alter the fact.

The usual precision of reference is to be demanded for the next item of Paul's six injunctions, "whatsoever things are just." To assume that the reference is to righteousness is not specific enough. In the everyday ethic of Epicurus the meaning of justice was obedience to the law of the land. In one context we find him writing: "Let us do everything honorably according to the laws." In Romans 13:1 Paul writes: "Let every person be subject to the governing authorities." Epicurus writes: "The laws are enacted for the sake of the wise, not that they may do wrong, but to prevent them from suffering wrong." Paul writes in Romans 13:3: "For rulers are not a deterrent to good behavior but to bad."

These quotations demonstrate plainly that the attitude of Paul toward the civil authorities is practically identical with that of Epicurus, but, as usual, the motivation is different. In this chapter of Romans Paul takes the position that "the powers that be are ordained of God" and that "love is the fulfilling of the law." In the last analysis, according to him, the Christian obeys the law "because love worketh no ill to his neighbor."

Neither was the motivation of Epicurus coldly utilitarian. His biographer speaks of his patriotic attitude toward his country as "beyond words to describe." If in his candor he often mentioned the motive of expediency, we must also remember that the most honorable action may also be profitable.

In respect of this question of obedience to the law the procedure of Paul himself deserves to be scanned. In spite of the fact that in First Thessalonians 5:3 he poured contempt upon the catchwords of Peace and Safety, he was by no means blind to the wisdom of the Epicurean practice. For himself he did not pursue safety; at times it was his deliberate choice not to seek protection for himself as a Roman citizen: he submitted to scourging under Roman law just as he had submitted to flogging under Jewish law. For the members of his churches, on the contrary, he coveted the blessings of peace and safety. He encouraged for them no cult of martyrdom any more than Epicurus encouraged it for his followers. It was after his time, though immediately afterward, that the leaders of Christianity began to find reason for the defiance of Roman law.

Only one of Paul's six injunctions now awaits explanation: "whatsoever things are true." This, like the others, may be redeemed from its present vagueness by recourse to the precepts of Epicurus. He required of his disciples total truthfulness in personal relations. This virtue was to be seasoned with courtesy, not peppered with censure, as with the Stoics. Expressed in Latin, where it is well authenticated, the ideal was *comitas* with *severitas*, a kindly courtesy joined with unflinching veracity. It was for this combination of traits that Atticus, the Epicurean friend of Cicero, was praised; his biographer writes of him that "it was hard to decide whether his friends feared or loved him more."

Commendable as this union of courtesy with veracity may seem to be, it still falls short of describing the whole meaning of truthfulness according to Epicurus. Veracity must be demanded as well as practiced. Of the Epicurean Atticus it is recorded: "He would neither be guilty of telling a lie nor of submitting to listen to one." Is it then likely that Paul was demanding less when he wrote in Colossians 3:9: "Do not lie to one another," and in Galatians 6:1: "Brethren, if a man is overtaken in some misdoing, you who are spiritual should set him right in a spirit of gentleness"?

It is hard to escape the conclusion that all three aspects of truthfulness are in the mind of Paul: to speak the truth, to demand that others speak the truth, and to correct the friend without condemning him.

Incidentally, the words *gentle* and *gentleness* seem to have been overworked in our translations of the New Testament. They are not specific enough. For instance, in the sentence above it would be more precise to read "a spirit of considerateness." The Epicurean combination of truthfulness with a considerate courtesy undoubtedly attracted Paul. In Ephesians 4:15 he calls it "speaking the truth in love."

If now we pause and survey these findings and set them in order, it will appear that the rhythm of this sententious verse, as we have come to know it in the King James Version, has been sacrificed, but by way of compensation the true significance of each item has been fixed with precision and the reference of all to the appropriate area of conduct has been defined. The residue may be worded as follows in plain prose: "Finally, brethren, everything that promotes truthfulness, everything that promotes reverence, everything that promotes respect for law, everything that promotes chastity, everything that promotes friendliness, everything that promotes charity in speech, whatever virtue there be, whatever be worthy of praise, think on these things."

32

## Think on These Things

Out of our prosaic version submitted above it has been thought worth while to reserve for closer scrutiny the final injunction of Paul, "think on these things." In these innocent words we shall find something more than meets the eye. To this formula of writing the reading public of the time had long been habituated by the textbooks of Epicurus. For example, he concludes the hortatory letter to the lad Menoeceus with the advice, "Meditate upon these things."

A rewarding clue may be found in the verb employed by Paul. It is more colorful than *think*. It has been taken over from the domain of arithmetic and means "to do figuring" or, we may say, "to calculate," because the ancients used pebbles in counting. The word *calculus* means "pebble" in Latin.

This verb signifying "to calculate" is often used by Paul; it does not occur in the Gospels but is a favorite of Epicurus. For instance, he recommends to the lad Menoeceus the practice of "sober calculation, which searches out the reasons for deciding to do or not to do any particular thing." In another context he puts the same advice in a different shape, saying in effect: "What will be the result for me if I choose to do this and what will be the result if I choose not to do it?"

To illustrate by an imaginary example: "This sumptuous meal will make me ill but my stomach hankers for it. Will the pleasure be worth the pain?" Modern critics have disdainfully dubbed this "the calculus of pleasure" but more precisely it may be called "the calculus of advantage." In this same letter to Menoeceus Epicurus writes: "The proper procedure in all actions is to scan the advantages and the disadvantages and weigh them against each other."

This calculus of advantage under the name of expediency is in bad odor today and has been seized upon to justify the denunciation of Epicurus as an "egoistic hedonist," actuated solely by self-interest. This charge, however, will not bear a moment's scrutiny. Epicurus came very close to enunciating the Golden Rule and declares in one of his best-known Authorized Doctrines that a man cannot live pleasurably unless honorably, that is, in accordance with the unwritten laws that govern the conduct of a gentleman. In another saying he warns a young man who was prone to sexual indulgence against "causing distress to a neighbor" and in this context he was expressly stating the principle of expediency.

This topic was a familiar ingredient of public knowledge in Paul's time and he reveals ample awareness of it, employing the same terminology as Epicurus. He is also at one with Epicurus in understanding expediency as the good of one's neighbor. For instance, he writes in First Corinthians 10:23–24: "All things are permissible for me but all things are not expedient; all things are permissible for me but not all things are edifying. Let no man seek his own good but the good of the other man." Both he and Epicurus conceive of advantage or expediency as being a reciprocal thing, the parties to the action being mutually benefited.

It will consequently be justifiable, when Paul writes "think on these things," to infer that his meaning is definite and specific, that he is encouraging his readers to make a practice of striking a balance between the advantages, for example, of speaking charitably of others and the disadvantages of speaking maliciously, or between the advantages of showing one's self friendly and the disadvantages of discourtesy and surliness.

We should next observe that this technique of meditation, measuring the gains of virtue against the costs of vice, conduces to peace of mind in the individual and peace in the community. This boon of peace in both its aspects was a chief objective of Epicurus no less than of Paul; but Paul cannot afford to appear to be in debt to philosophy, much less to Epicurus. He consequently ignores his predecessor even while building upon the foundation he had laid and concludes with the words, "and the God of peace will be with you."

The philosophy of peace is in process of being replaced by the religion of peace.

## In Whatsoever State I Am

There is a definite irony in the fact that Paul should have hurled at the Epicureans the taunt of making a god of the belly and then wind up his letter with the topic of self-control in matters of eating, revealing that his teaching is up to a certain point identical with that of Epicurus. The words in which he sums up his doctrine, "in whatsoever state I am, therewith to be content," hold equally valid as summing up the creed of his competitor.

The King James Version, however, was "appointed to be read in churches" and the instructions of the translators were to produce a

34

book of devotion, in which they succeeded magnificently. For this use their version is irreplaceable but for the purpose of study a more precise rendering is needed. To attain this end it becomes consequently necessary to sacrifice the euphony for the sake of the precision which was previously sacrificed for the sake of the euphony.

The topic of self-control in eating and drinking was a hackneyed one and the key word in the discussions was *autarkes,* here translated as "content," though "self-sufficient" would be more exact. It is used by many philosophers, Epicurus not excepted, but in the New Testament only by Paul. A quick glance at the history of the idea will be in order. To Diogenes the Cynic self-sufficiency signified independence of all the amenities of life, including food, clothing, and shelter, and he chose to sleep in an overturned wine cask, as if in a kennel. Against this beastliness the gentlemanly Epicurus rebelled with vigor and he defined the word anew to mean independence of all changes of fortune, such as from riches to poverty or freedom to slavery, along with the compulsions and privations that attend them.

Even in a brief statement of his teaching may be discerned the repudiation of Diogenes: "And self-sufficiency we believe to be a great good, not that we may live on little under all circumstances, but that we may be content with little when we do not have much."

With this judgment Paul was in total accord. He saw no intrinsic merit in stinting one's self systematically nor any demerit in eating heartily when plenty was available. The merit consisted in being prepared to adapt one's self to circumstances. Neither did this readiness to adapt one's self, either in his case or in that of Epicurus, mean resigning one's self. In either event, plenty or want, the man was equally master of himself, always under self-control. Paul knows the regular Greek term for self-control, and uses it once, Galatians 5:23; it denotes a "fruit of the Spirit." It is not found in the Gospels.

The question of riches and contentment is briefly discussed by Paul in First Timothy 6:6–10, where a knowledge of Epicureanism will clarify the meaning and improve the translation, which in the Revised Standard is somewhat obscure and ambiguous, as in verse 6: "There is great gain in godliness with contentment." Paul is not intending us to believe that contentment results in a "gain in godliness." The clue to the meaning is to be found in a famous saying of Epicurus, excerpted from a letter to a patron who was financing the studies of a lad Pythocles: "If you wish to make Pythocles really rich, do not add to the money, but subtract from his desires."

This is a paradox and we must concentrate sharply to grasp it. Another saying of Epicurus will help: "Nothing is enough for a man for whom enough is too little." In other words, the adequacy of income varies with the desires; as the desires diminish the income may be said to increase.

We must now concentrate again to read this meaning into Paul's words. He first speaks of evil men who "think godliness a means of increasing their income." To this he retorts: "Godliness joined with self-sufficiency means an amazing increase of income." Instead of "self-sufficiency" translators have accustomed us to read "contentment" and to this there is no objection as long as we understand it to mean "contentment with little," concerning which Cicero informs us that "no one had more to say than Epicurus."

This is one of several instances where a passage much preferred as a devotional reading is Epicurean in both subject and sentiment. The Greek term for "self-sufficiency" or "contentment with little" occurs only here in the New Testament.

With all these facts kept well in mind and the willingness to sacrifice the euphonious liberties of the King James Version for the sake of precision, verses 11–12 may be rendered as follows: "Not that I speak of not having enough, for I have learned to content myself with the conditions in which I find myself; I know how to humble myself and I know how to restrain myself when there is more than enough; under any and all conditions I understand how to eat my fill and how to endure hunger, and likewise how to act when there is more than enough and how to content myself when there is less than enough."

Beyond this point Paul is no longer in accord with Epicurus and, as usual, the necessity of their parting can be traced to the motivation. Epicurus was perpetuating the time-honored assumption of the rational Greeks that virtue is knowledge, though he invokes his own version of this principle, that is, the calculus of advantage. He carefully lists the advantages that accrue to the side of moderation and these may be quoted in summary: "It is conducive to health; it enables the individual to face unflinchingly the vicissitudes of life; it disposes men to exercise better judgment when rich foods become available after intervals of scarcity; lastly, it renders men dauntless in the face of Fortune."

In this seemingly unimpeachable pronouncement the lurking fallacy in Paul's judgment is the assumption that right reason is a guarantee of right action. What the system lacks is the dynamic element, some power to ensure that the individual will possess the resolution to do what reason has judged to be advantageous. This tacit criticism is contained in verse 13: "I can do all things in him who strengthens me."

It may be questioned, however, whether this translation is the best possible. If allowance be made for Greek idiom a new version may be ventured for the sake of locating the emphasis where it is needed: "There is nothing I lack the power to do through him who puts his strength into me."

If now a moment may be spared for a rapid survey, we shall have discovered Paul to be reasoning at times after the fashion of Epicurus; we shall have observed the employment of certain words that are peculiar to the vocabularies of Epicurus and Paul; we shall have found several topics to have been illuminated for us by citation of the teachings of Epicurus; and in particular, we shall have found the euphonious verse beginning "whatsoever things are true" to be completely redeemed from its present vagueness by knowledge of Epicurean precepts.

One item of information may also be mentioned for future reflection: Paul seems to display far too much affinity with the cheerful and friendly Epicureans to have ever been enamored of the censorious Stoics, who revered as their founder "the sour and scowling Zeno."

# III

# THESSALONIANS

## Peace and Safety

WHILE the chief topic of this Epistle will be Peace and Safety we shall learn something worth while about Paul by calling Epicurus to testify concerning the question of honesty, which arises in First Thessalonians 2:1–8.

In the Revised Standard it is made to begin: "For you yourselves know, brethren, that our visit to you was not in vain." We believe this to be wrong and that this error has beclouded the interpretation and translation of the whole paragraph, which consequently calls for fresh scrutiny. We believe the true meaning to be, "our visit to you was not a sham" or a "pretense." Paul will be found to be defending himself against the charge of duplicity, as he also does elsewhere.

The clue to a correct interpretation, as often happens, may be found in a word that Paul shares with Epicurus. It is the verb *parresiazomai* (2:2), which in the New Testament occurs only in Acts and in two Pauline Epistles. In the Revised Standard it is rendered "we had courage" and in the best New Testament lexicon it is defined "to speak freely or boldly, be bold in speech." This definition is not incorrect for classical Greek but in the philosophy of Epicurus the word was slightly deflected to signify "speak with absolute frankness or truthfulness."

Absolute veracity was a fetish with Epicurus and, as usual, it was part of his structure of thought. His teachings were later amplified by the Epicurean Philodemus of Gadara under the title *On Frankness*, a work still extant in extensive fragments. From these may be gleaned much information on the topic of admonition, of which the Epicureans preceded Paul in making a specialty. It is likely that Paul knew the treatise at first hand.

Even the teaching of Epicurus himself can be documented to a certain extent and it possesses intrinsic value, quite apart from the help it affords in arriving at Paul's meaning.

As elsewhere mentioned in this study, Epicurus rejected the Platonic reason as the norm of truth and exalted Nature in its stead. Nature, he insisted, was honest herself and demanded honesty of her devotees. To be dishonest or untruthful was deemed unworthy of a student of natural phenomena; for a scientist to lie about his observations would be a sort of treason. This is implied in a saying of his: "As for me, I should prefer to speak with absolute honesty, as befits the study of nature, and utter oracular sayings beneficial to all men, even if not a soul shall understand me, rather than, by falling into line with popular opinions, to reap the lush praise that falls from the favor of the multitude."

With this contempt of popular favor Paul could fully concur and he reveals his feeling in this very paragraph, verse 6: "nor did we seek glory from men, either from you or from others."

In another saying Epicurus writes: "I was never ambitious to please the multitude." In this same paragraph Paul writes, verse 4: "so we speak, not to please men," though he makes the customary change of motivation, "but to please God, who scrutinizes our hearts." This is characteristic of Paul's use of sentiments taken from Epicurus: he changes the motivation; in this instance he substitutes loyalty to God for loyalty to Nature, whom Epicurus the scientist revered as the supreme teacher.

Still other echoes of Epicurus may be delved out of this engaging paragraph, which amply deserves to be redeemed from its present obscurity. However surprising it may seem to be, this man Epicurus, who was reputed to be an enemy of religion, shared with Jesus a reverence for little children. He did not, it is true, believe them to be born sinless, because the word *sin* was not in his vocabulary, but he did believe them to be born honest and sincere, though often defiled later by education. For example, if children should have been given such an education as to lead them to suppose that happiness was to be derived from wealth or fame, they would have been defiled. They would have erred from the truth and become unclean.

The knowledge of this teaching will now enable us to apprehend the exact significance of verse 3 of our paragraph, which is decidedly vague in the Revised Standard: "For our appeal does not spring from error

39

or uncleanness." At a slight sacrifice of brevity this may be rendered precise by reading: "For our appeal does not have its origin in an aberration from honesty or from impure motives."

If Paul had either sought favor by flattery or been possessed of a desire for gain which he sought to conceal, his motives would have been impure according to Epicurus, nor would he have been following the straight path of honesty. It is against these very imputations that Paul defends himself, in verse 5: "For never did we use either words of flattery, as you know, or a cloak for gain."

Epicurus the helper may be invoked to assist in correcting still another error in this darkened paragraph, verse 7, which in the Revised Standard reads in part: "But we were gentle among you, like a nurse taking care of her children." It is the word *gentle* that strikes a false note: the word *babes* has been used in its stead and is closer to the Greek. The key to the true meaning may be found in two items of Epicurean teaching: first, that children are honest unless spoiled, as already mentioned; and second, that the good teacher or nurse will also be honest, that is, actuated solely by the good of the child. Hence the meaning must be: "But we came among you guileless as a child, just as a nurse is guileless in caring for the children given to her charge." The correctness of this is confirmed in verse 11, "like a father with his children," the good father being free from self-interest and actuated solely by the good of the children.

The pagan Epicurus, though a convinced celibate like Paul, displayed a keen discernment in matters of family life. The two men, in spite of the chasm that separated the logic of the atom from the logic of the cross, thought remarkably alike on domestic matters.

Before assembling the corrections already made it remains to make a minor improvement in verses 6–7, which in the Revised Standard read in part as follows: "nor did we seek glory from men, neither from you nor from others, though we might have made demands as apostles of Christ." It is this last clause that falls short of being precise.

The key word of the Greek text is associated with vainglorious kings who pitch their voices low to impress their subjects and with pretentious actors who do the same in performing kingly roles. Epicurus used to twit the Platonists with putting on similar airs; in point of fact they bore the reputation of being the highsteppers among the philosophers. The last clause in the sentence above may consequently be rendered: "though we might have assumed the grand manner as apostles of Christ." Paul means to say that he might well have made a bid for glory.

It remains now to readjust our understanding of the whole paragraph in the light of these findings. Paul is manifestly defending himself against the charge of having been animated by self-interest. It is for this reason that the words "our visit was not in vain" must be changed to read "our visit was not a sham."

It is equally necessary to emend the words that follow: "we had courage in our God to declare to you the gospel." To mention courage is tempting in English but the Greeks did not call moral courage by the same name as physical courage. The question here is rather one of honesty or dishonesty, sincerity or pretense. The manhandling suffered by Paul at Philippi might have been thought to tempt him to appease the Thessalonicans by flattery; it might, he hints, have deflected him from that absolute honesty, which he, like Epicurus before him, esteemed to be of paramount consequence. What he writes may therefore be rendered more precisely: "but notwithstanding the fact that in Philippi we had been assaulted and subjected to shameful indignities, as you well know, still, with the help of our God, we spoke the absolute truth in declaring to you the gospel of God under great stress."

## Peace and Safety

Among the numerous clues that serve to identify references to the Epicureans none is more specific and certain than the mention of their watchwords Peace and Safety. These occur in First Thessalonians 5:3, where the King James Version runs: "For when they shall say, Peace and Safety, then sudden destruction cometh upon them." This falls far short of exactitude but it is superior to the Revised Standard: "When people say, 'There is peace and security,' then sudden destruction will come upon them."

The unlucky change from "when they shall say" to "when people say" is based upon the gratuitous assumption that no particular group or sect is being singled out for censure but merely some section of the populace that refuses to be alarmed by the prediction of the second coming and the destruction of unbelievers. The perplexity of translators is due to the fact that catchwords of unmistakable reference in Paul's time have lost their significance through the lapse of the centuries.

41

No person of ordinary intelligence at the date when the letter was written would have been ignorant that peace and safety were objectives of the Epicurean way of life. Recognition of this fact will enable us to correct the translation. To this end it must be remembered that the second coming and the destruction of unbelievers are events in the future but the threat is present and perpetual. With this knowledge kept well in mind we shall be able to set the tenses to rights: "At the very moment that they are saying 'peace and safety' sudden destruction is hanging over them."

When once this identification of the Epicureans has been made, confirmation will be the more certain in the seemingly innocent words (4:3), "the others who have no hope." This signifies no hope of benefiting by the grace of God and the Epicureans were so characterized even outside of the New Testament by their rivals the Stoics, because they denied divine providence.

Additional confirmation of a new and oblique sort will be found in the Second Epistle, 2:1–12, where the coming of Antichrist is predicted. It has long since been observed that the description admirably fits the character of the notorious Antiochus Epiphanes, king of Syria and persecutor of the Jews. What has not been so well known is the fact that this king became a convert to the creed of Epicurus and adopted it as the court philosophy. Thus the ominous inference is forced upon us that Epicureanism is to be associated with Antichrist.

This outline of evidence will now be amplified.

## Peace

Any lingering doubt that peace was a watchword of the Epicureans may be set at rest by the testimony of St. Augustine, who at one time was tempted to become an adherent of the sect and long remained partial toward it. In one passage he characterized them by three words: Pleasure, Suavity, and Peace. It is quite true that he lived three centuries later than Paul but his word is still good for the earlier date; the creed of Epicurus was notorious for tenacity of doctrine. Later Epicureans, such as Philodemus, elaborated without altering the original teachings.

It will be helpful to observe that Peace has been coupled with Pleasure and Suavity. The Epicureans were men of good will and urbanity, "least of all malicious," as Cicero admitted. From the first they had taken care to differentiate themselves from the snarling Cynic philosophers, who went about insulting all and sundry and scorning the decencies of life; and not less from the Stoics, a censorious sect who condemned all pleasure and made a virtue of being disagreeable.

This aversion from Cynics and Stoics, along with the emphasis upon good will and brotherly love, had its sequel later on in a marked similarity between Epicureans and Christians, embarrassing to Paul and repelling and attracting him alternately. He was also betrayed into inconsistency. For example, in these very Epistles to the Thessalonians he writes in the salutation, "Grace to you and *peace*," and in 5:3 this same word is used with scorn when he writes "peace and safety."

Furthermore, it is no formality when he adds, "from God the Father and the Lord Jesus Christ." It must never be overlooked that this salutation was an innovation. It was invented by Paul for Christian use. Epicurus himself, who instituted the custom of composing epistles for colonies of disciples, had shown himself an innovator in this regard. The usual Greek salutation was "Rejoice," although it became so washed out with use as to mean no more than "Dear Sir." Epicurus varied it by such heartening phrases as "Live the good life" or "Put zest into living," it being his teaching that this life was the only life and should be enjoyed to the full.

Now Paul, adopting the custom of composing epistles for colonies of converts, was confronted by the necessity of choosing a new salutation for his particular needs. Neither does it require any exceptional acumen to discern that he took a suggestion from the mammon of unrighteousness, as Jesus had recommended. Not that he copied Epicurus; he imitated his example only so far as his new salutation should be an expression of good will. In substance he was repudiating the example of Epicurus but the example that is repudiated may have even more influence over a man's choice than the example that is adopted. One item that Paul deliberately chose to write into the new salutation was the doctrine of grace, which Epicurus, by persistently denying the interest of the gods in human affairs, had rendered indispensable for a living religion.

As for the word *peace* in Paul's salutation, the idea it embodied was incapable of being utterly different from the concept of peace according to Epicurus, who had won for it the status of a blessed aspiration in the public mind; what Paul did was to shift the idea to a new com-

43

plex of meanings, adding something to its content and modifying the motivation. The peace of mind that was long associated with Epicurus is transformed into the peace of God. Here again, philosophy is in process of being supplanted by religion.

A slight amplification will make this more clear. What especially repelled Paul was the claim of Epicurus that a man could achieve peace of mind by his own efforts. This is what Epicurus meant when he wrote: "It is silly to pray to the gods for things that a man is capable of obtaining for himself." The poet Horace, who often quotes Epicurean doctrine exactly, has this to say: "as for peace of mind, I'll provide that for myself." It is in opposition to this public teaching that Paul writes: "Grace to you and peace from God our Father and our Lord Jesus Christ."

In this connection still another point is worthy of mention. The disciples of Epicurus were known among themselves as "Friends of Epicurus." It was natural, therefore, for the master to address his epistles, for example, *To the Friends in Asia.* Paul avoids this word *friend* as if ill-omened and writes instead, for example, *To the saints and faithful brethren in Christ.* This too is a repudiation of Epicurus but it is also an imitation.

## Peace in the Family

A close scrutiny of this topic of peace will increase our understanding of the New Testament, because the Epicureans had made intensive studies of the topic in advance of Paul and their findings were part of the public knowledge of his time.

Peace of mind, to which the present study has been confined down to this point, was by Epicurus called *ataraxy*, which all our larger English dictionaries, copying one another, mistakenly define as "stoical indifference," confusing it with apathy. The Stoics feared the emotions and cultivated indifference; the friendly Epicurus had no fear of emotions in general, which he regarded as normal, but only of disturbing emotions, such as fear of the gods and death and judgment after death. These, he believed, could all be dispelled by a true understanding of the constitution of the universe, which to his thinking was a vast self-operating mechanism, in which man alone was master of his fate, unbothered by interfering gods.

It goes without saying that this frame of thought into which Epicurus had built this concept of peace was blasphemous to Paul's soul, nor could he demean himself by employing the word *ataraxy*. The Epicureans themselves, however, had made use of another word, *eirene*, to denote peace in the family and among neighbors. This more ordinary word is consequently made to serve in the Epistles, as in the New Testament generally, for both kinds of peace.

This phenomenon of an Epicurean word being dropped while its meaning was transferred to another is not exceptional. The Epicureans exalted brotherly love under the name of *philia*, which is replaced in the New Testament by *agape*, meaning the same thing. Another instance of such substitution is the Christian word *catachumens*, which signifies pupils being prepared for baptism and confirmation. This was a mere translation of an Epicurean term *kataskeuazomenoi*, signifying pupils in a preparatory school, i.e., those not yet ready for full "confirmation" in the new way of life. Here again, Epicureanism may be seen as anticipating Christian procedures.

The aspect of peace which stands closest to peace of mind, both being denoted by the same word in the New Testament, is peace within the family. Of this topic the Epicureans had made their usual studies and thereby obtained for certain homely virtues a status of importance which had been denied them by Plato, who confined his attention to political virtues, especially justice. The very word that to Plato signified justice must be rendered righteousness in the New Testament and this is typical of the shift of interest from political toward social virtues, to which Epicurus gave a powerful impulse.

It may be readily allowed that the study of the social virtues became a general trend among the philosophers who followed Plato in point of time, but Epicurus and his successors were singular among them in being conscious of the mission of promoting human happiness. Theirs was the only missionary philosophy produced by the Greeks. Their attitude was pragmatic; they were interested in practical problems of conduct. Consequently it was quite natural that they should adopt their own characteristic scheme of arrangement in their treatment of virtues.

It was their choice to draw up lists of "vices and the corresponding virtues." In this there is a sound logic; the vice can be defined only as the opposite of the virtue. Without the vice, the corresponding virtue would possess no meaning. For example, if we could imagine a society in which there was not a single liar, then there would be no praise for truthfulness; it would cease to be a virtue.

This device of opposing the vice to the virtue was taken over by Paul without any concealment; his attitude toward religion was no less pragmatic than that of Epicurus toward philosophy. The truth is that he elaborates the device and incorporates it with amazing ingenuity into his new spiritual structure of doctrine. It is such elaboration that we should discern in the closing passage of Galatians, where he discourses upon "the desires of the Spirit" and "the desires of the flesh," and "the works of the Spirit" and "the works of the flesh." No small part of the charm of First Corinthians 13 depends upon the use of this ethical counterpoint as a literary expedient: "Love is patient and kind; love is *not* jealous or boastful; it is *not* arrogant or rude." A veritable garland of examples is found in this passage.

While other examples may be garnered from various Epistles, the particular virtues that make for peace and harmony in family life receive chief emphasis in the closing passages of Ephesians and Colossians, where Paul offers wise counsel to husbands, wives, children, slaves, and masters. More awaits to be said when these Epistles come under discussion; here it will suffice to call attention to the list of vices that mar the peace of the family and the community — anger, wrath, malice, slander, and foul talk — and the opposing virtues that make for peace — compassion, kindness, lowliness, meekness, and patience.

It is always well to pause for a surveying glance: here it may occur to the mind how easily a good Epicurean family might have become a good Christian family; their codes of morals were very similar; the structure of doctrine needed to be changed, as also the motivation, but not the precepts.

## Safety

No external evidence need be adduced to certify the status of safety as a watchword of the Epicureans. The word itself occurs in four of the forty Authorized Doctrines of the founder and the idea behind it is elaborated in at least five others.

The teaching there embodied possesses singular importance because it can be traced down through history to the Declaration of Independence and the American Constitution. This influence has completely escaped the acumen of historians, just as the influence of Epicurus upon

Paul has escaped the notice of New Testament scholars, and for this reason a brief glance at the story may be justified.

Plato had devoted the greater part of his thought to the topic of justice, which to the Greeks was almost synonymous with government — an alternative title to Plato's *Republic* is *On Justice* — and arrived at the conclusion that citizens should be tightly controlled in a closed society resembling modern communistic states. Epicurus, always hostile to Plato, advocated an open society with a minimum of government.

He rejected the Platonic dialectic as a means of discovering truth and set up Nature as the teacher. To discover what justice really is, he asserted, it is sufficient to observe a herd of wild animals, elephants probably preferred. They do not injure one another and they organize themselves to protect one another. This is "the justice of Nature," and he condensed it to one sentence in Authorized Doctrine 31: "The justice of Nature is a covenant of advantage to the end that men shall not injure one another nor be injured."

Safety to him, therefore, signified the security of the individual against injury to his person, assuming that this would be useless unless his property were also protected. John Locke took over this idea from Epicurus but he dared not mention the alleged enemy of religion as his source, because he was writing in the age of the Puritans. He also disguised the principle by reversing it; he declared the function of government to be the protection of the property of the citizen, assuming it to be useless to protect his property unless his person were also protected.

Thomas Jefferson, however, one of the few men with courage to avow himself an Epicurean, reversed this reversal; the words he wrote into the Declaration of Independence were not "property, liberty, and the pursuit of wealth" but "life, liberty, and the pursuit of happiness," veritable watchwords of Epicureanism.

If this little digression shall have enhanced our respect for Epicurus, we may feel less reluctance to recognize the evidences of his reasonings in the thought of Paul.

The fact that safety was a catchword in Paul's time, even apart from the writings of Epicurus, is amply evidenced by the policy of the Roman government under which he lived. This government was earning a singular fame for itself by the fidelity with which it undertook to protect the persons of its citizens. The lengths to which it was willing to go to this end, if once appealed to, is exemplified by the protection afforded Paul himself when attacked in Jerusalem. He was furnished an escort of seventy horsemen all the way to Caesarea and an additional guard of four hundred infantry for the more dangerous stage of the journey (Acts 23:23 and 32).

On this topic of safety and the Roman government something may yet be added. The assurance of safety and peace was denoted by the word *securitas* and this began to become a catchword in Cicero's lifetime. A century later, in the days of Nero, under whom Paul was martyred, it received full recognition and began to appear upon imperial coins as a deity, SECURITAS.

## Paul and Safety

Paul's attitude toward the problem of personal safety was not the same at all periods of his ministry and deserves to be traced. It will turn out to be very different from that of Epicurus.

In his earlier ministry it is doubtful whether Paul could have spoken contemptuously of safety, as he did in First Thessalonians 5:3. It can hardly be doubted that the question of safety was a factor in deterring him from entering Bithynia and the Roman province of Asia (Acts 16:6–7). Quite rightly he judged that the safest place for him was a synagogue or at least a place of prayer, as at Philippi (Acts 16:13), because both Greeks and Romans were tolerant of foreign religions so long as adherents confined their activities to premises of their own. Again, when forced to leave Philippi, he decided it was prudent not to stop at Amphipolis and Apollonia, going instead to Thessalonica, where there was a synagogue (Acts 17:1).

At this stage of his experience Paul was still allowing his friends to make decisions for him. It was they who spirited him out of Thessalonica and later out of Beroea (Acts 17:10 and 14–15), furnishing him an escort to Athens.

This episode of Paul's visit to Athens falls under this topic of safety, though its significance has become obscured by the belief that he spoke on Mars' Hill. This hill is almost three hundred feet above the market place and distant a good half-hour's walk by a steep climb. No plausible reason can be discovered for such an effort having been demanded of the apostle.

Mars' Hill is an unfortunate translation of the Greek word Areopagus, which was also the name of a court and a courtroom. What happened was that the philosophers escorted Paul into this courtroom, which was close by the spot where he had been speaking. He was under suspicion. In the synagogue he had been free to speak as he pleased but to become "a preacher of foreign divinities" in public was to invite trouble.

Similarly, when he had finished the recorded speech in the courtroom, the words of Acts 17:32, "We will hear you again about this," were an unveiled threat, a virtual adjournment of the hearing. This was the interpretation placed upon the words by Paul and he went on to Corinth "in much fear and trembling," in spite of the original plan to await the arrival of Silas and Timothy.

It is consequently manifest that only gradually the conviction forced itself upon Paul that to pursue safety and to preach the gospel were incompatible. This meant the discovery of the merit that lay in the suffering of persecution, a discovery that Jesus had made before him. It forced Paul to the decision that he would not avail himself of the protection due to him as a Roman citizen. Had he not reached this decision, there would have been no need for him to submit five times to flogging under Jewish law, much less to three scourgings with rods under Roman law, of which we learn in Second Corinthians 11:24–25.

It followed that by the compulsion of experience he was forced to adopt one policy for himself and recommend another for his converts. As a first consideration of safety he urged upon the latter obedience to the law, as in Romans 13:1: "Let every person be subject to the governing authorities." As for himself, he was convinced that his status as a preacher of the gospel would be impaired by the pursuit of safety and this status enhanced by submission to persecution. Had he regularly exercised his right to appeal to Rome for protection, he could no longer have boasted as he does in Second Corinthians 11:21–27.

It may be added that when on trial before Festus he said, "I appeal to Caesar," it was not safety he sought or justice; it was the opportunity of going to Rome in custody, which seemed to be the only feasible way of satisfying his desire to visit that city.

## Epicurus and Safety

The ultimate attitude of Epicurus toward personal safety was also founded upon experience of persecution but it was his choice to pursue safety as a policy, which renders understandable the scorn of Paul. This scorn became the more justified in later days, after persecutions had become frequent, and St. Basil is referring to Epicureans without naming them when he writes somewhat icily of those "who place a higher value upon nothing than upon truth and safety."

Epicurus, of course, lived and died before the eastern Mediterranean had come under Roman rule and his precepts were framed for the Greek world to which he belonged. As a primary assurance of safety he recommended to his disciples, just as Paul did later, to be obedient to the laws of the land.

The courts of law, he well knew, though ostensibly existing for the sake of justice, were only too often employed as an agency of envy to rob the rich of their wealth, politicians of their power, and famous men of their prestige. The obscure citizen was the safest. It was consequently his general advice "to live and die unknown," and in particular "to shun the political career."

To round off the picture of society as he knew it, we should also remember that except in the largest cities there was no police protection. Each individual was responsible for his own safety. To this end Epicurus exalted friendship as the surest guarantee. The making of friends was too important to be left to chance. In one of his Authorized Doctrines he recommended "to make all relationships friendly where possible; where this was not possible, to render them at least not unfriendly; and where not even this was possible, to avoid contacts." It was to avoid contacts that he confined his teaching to his garden in Athens.

In spite of this systematic pursuit of safety, the good Epicurean was not by any means a shameless sponsor of safety at any price. Long before Jesus is reported to have said, "Greater love hath no man than this, that a man lay down his life for his friends," Epicurus had written: "The wise man will on occasion die for a friend."

This view was reasoned out in a characteristic way, which may be read in another saying: "Nothing can be terrible to a man while living if there is nothing terrible to him in not living." In other words, if a man has no fear of death, because it is an eternity of unconsciousness, neither will he fear the tyrant or his torture. In yet another saying, this Epicurus, whom a great scholar has seen fit to disparage as a "moral invalid," anticipates the resolution of the Christian martyr: "The wise man, even on the rack, is a happy man."

## Epicurean and Pauline Admonition

It is both astonishing and informing to discover Paul adopting the procedures of the capable but irritating Epicureans in this same fifth chapter of the first Epistle to the Thessalonians which begins with the prediction of their destruction. We should observe and keep in mind his addiction to the words *admonish* and *admonition*. Except for one example in Acts, these are confined to the Epistles of Paul and with the Epicureans they were technical. The sect made a specialty of ethical instruction, which they styled "a many-sided art." By *admonition* was meant "suggestion" or "correction without blame or reprimand."

Over and above the friendly and uncondemning tone, which Paul in Ephesians 4:15 calls "speaking the truth in love" — a tone which he sometimes found it hard to maintain — we should observe also the content of the advice and exhortation. A few parallels between Paul's advice and that of Epicurus may be presented item by item.

Epicurus planned that his philosophy of life should be independent of tutors, extending itself by mutual instruction and admonition. Paul writes, verse 11: "Therefore encourage one another and build one another up, just as you are doing."

Epicurus urged the value of reverence, "a great good to the one who feels the reverence," especially reverence for those more advanced in wisdom. Paul writes, verse 12: "And we beseech you, brethren, to respect those who labor among you and are over you in the Lord and admonish you."

It is true that Epicurus saw little value in prayer but he did declare that continuous happiness was possible and he exalted the virtue of gratitude to first rank as a factor of happiness. Verse 16 is therefore partly Epicurean, partly exclusively Pauline: "Rejoice always, pray constantly, give thanks under all circumstances."

If doubt exists that Paul in this Epistle had Epicurean admonition in mind, this can be dispelled by his warning about "quenching the Spirit." This was the effect, as he pondered the matter, of "despising prophecy." To understand this it is necessary to recall the statement of Cicero concerning Epicurus: "There was nothing he ridiculed so much as the prediction of future events." Hence 5:19 and 20: "Quench not the Spirit. Despise not prophesyings." To ridicule the prediction of the second coming in particular was to Paul's way of thinking "quenching the Spirit."

The clue to the last item in this list is the most likely of all to escape detection. Epicurus made a cardinal virtue of total honesty. Of the wise man, who corresponds to the saint in Christian thought, he writes that "he will be the same in his slumbers." Even in sleep, when the evil in human nature is prone to reassert itself, the truly good man will be the same as in waking hours. Is this not the meaning of Paul when he writes in verse 10: "so that whether we wake or sleep we might live with him"? What was total honesty to Epicurus becomes in Paul's structure of ethic total sanctification.

A momentous addition, however, remains to be made. The diligent student of Paul's thought may have observed a minor device of his writing: in a casual way he drops the hint of a certain sentiment and after an interval returns to it with amplification. In this instance the hint may be discerned in verse 10, quoted above, and the amplification is found in verse 23, next to the last, a fitting climax to this ladder of admonition. Total sanctification, the substitute for the total honesty of Epicurus, is the theme: "May the God of peace himself sanctify you *wholly*; and may your spirits and your souls be preserved *in their integrity* and your bodies be guarded *blamelessly* at the coming of the Lord Jesus Christ."

The above translation is our own. We regret at all times to depart from the euphonious words of the King James or other versions but for the present study the objective is precision. Perhaps it may be possible at times to obtain euphony also.

In this chapter we see in closer combination than elsewhere the repulsion and the attraction of Epicureanism, the ridicule of divine events that repelled and the kindly ethic that attracted. Paul builds upon the latter while vigorously condemning the former. He may be discerned in the very process of transforming an Epicurean community into a Christian community and Greek philosophy into the Christian religion, replacing, for example, the virtue of total honesty by the virtue of total sanctification.

The astonishing thing is the absence of mention of teachings of Jesus. This, however, becomes less astonishing when we recall that the Gospels were not yet available. It is not even certain, it may even be improbable, that Paul was familiar with the sayings of Jesus; he does not reason in the way that Jesus did nor teach after the manner of his teaching. It is certain, on the contrary, that he knew the precepts of

52

Epicurus and how to reason after his fashion. This will be amply demonstrated in the study of First Corinthians.

In the meantime we may pause to discern two distinct stages in the progress of Christian education, the first being based upon the sermons and Epistles of Paul, the next being based also upon Gospels, both those we possess and others that are lost, which must have been compiled for the express purpose of supplying the texts of instruction that were previously lacking. The Epicureans, on the contrary, had long been furnished with suitable textbooks and not unnaturally Paul drew upon these for his material, both because they were familiar to his Greek converts and because they were familiar to himself.

## Epicurus and Antichrist

In the second Epistle to the Thessalonians the main topic is the second coming. The prophecy of this event seems to have given rise to two parties who occasioned vexation to Paul and the other apostles: first, those who were prone to believe or easily incited to believe that the coming was imminent; and second, those who teased and bantered the Christians about the delay in the coming.

The teasers were the Epicureans. A well-reasoned caution against their activities may be found in Second Peter 3. The reasoning of Paul to the same end is less happy. He explains that the rebellion must come first and the man of lawlessness be revealed, who for the time being is being restrained. This is Antichrist, though the name is not used.

The concept of Antichrist, though of course not the name, was Jewish and oriental and hardly a fruitful one for the Christian tradition. It gave rise to protracted and useless speculation concerning the identity of "the man of lawlessness." It deserves consideration in this present study, however, because the description of the monster fits so admirably the known character of the notorious Antiochus Epiphanes, king of Syria from 174 to 167 B.C., who was a convert to Epicureanism.

His conversion to this creed became known through the publication of a mutilated papyrus document some fifty years ago but the information so revealed has not as yet been recognized as possessing a bearing upon the New Testament story.

According to this papyrus a learned Epicurean philosopher named Philonides resolved to make a convert of the king and began to ply him with letters and pamphlets. This campaign was crowned with success. Philonides was welcomed to the royal court in Antioch and assigned a residence across the square from the palace; this seems to have been ample for housing "a throng of scholars," who accompanied him.

These honors seem to have been fully deserved. The new favorite was employed as ambassador, and decrees in his honor have been found carved on stone at Athens and Delphi. He was later appointed to the governorship of a city. As a scholar he was enterprising. He published more than a hundred books, among them an edition of the letters of Epicurus and his chief collaborators; he also busied himself with collecting the writings of the Epicureans for the royal library.

These facts possess tremendous interest for the reason that they inform us of Antioch's having been an outstanding center of Epicureanism long before it became a center of Christianity. It was there, as Luke informs us in Acts 11:26, that the disciples of Jesus were first called Christians. Neither can much doubt exist that this name was coined for them to distinguish them from the disciples of Epicurus. We should bear steadily in mind that these two sects were singular in being named for their founders. We should also bear in mind that the disciples of Epicurus did not call one another Epicureans and the disciples of Jesus did not call themselves Christians. These names were coined by outsiders, possibly by members of the Roman colony in Antioch.

The information about Antioch possesses the more interest because this king Antiochus made himself the archenemy of the Jews. His very title Epiphanes, which means "god manifest," must have been odious to them, and he incurred their everlasting detestation by invading Judea and endeavoring to force Greek culture upon them. Neither can it be doubted, in view of his known conversion to Epicureanism, that his name was associated with this hated philosophy.

The inference is consequently justified that Paul, knowing the history of his race, could hardly have penned a description befitting Antiochus without thinking at the same time of Epicureanism.

## Scoffers in the Last Days

The assumption that the ridicule which aroused the indignation of Paul, as recorded in the Epistles to the Thessalonians, stemmed from the Epicureans meets with welcome and definite confirmation outside the Pauline writings in Second Peter 3, where the faithful are urged to "remember the predictions of the holy prophets." Verse 3 reads in part: "First of all you must understand this, that scoffers will come in the last days with scoffing."

But how, it may well be asked, can we be sure that these scoffers are to be identified as the disciples of Epicurus? In this instance the evidences are unusually abundant and follow hard upon one another.

The verse quoted in part above ends with these words, "following their own passions." This is slightly misleading and the King James even more so, "walking after their own lusts." It would be more exact to read, "walking according to their own desires." The point is that the sect of Epicurus stood out among all others as repudiating service or subjection to any divine being. It was they who above all others asserted the independence of man, who must be free to plan his whole life, uninhibited by fear of fate, fortune, or divine being; in their creed there was only scorn for such an injunction as "Thy will be done."

Epicurus even went so far as to think of man as emancipated from the rule of the laws of nature. In a universe dominated by natural law, according to him, man alone was exempt. The very atoms, he taught, swerved from their courses to allow him freedom of choice. He was free to choose evil and free to choose the good, because the gods were indifferent to human wickedness. Hence Epicureans are rightly described as "walking according to their own desires."

Now let us look at what follows. What do these scoffers say? They ask a question: "Where is the promise of his coming?" This is particularly revealing. The bantering question had been a specialty of Epicurus himself and he incurred persecution because of his skill at it. His disciples perpetuated the tradition. In Acts 17:18 they did not say that Paul was talking nonsense; they asked instead: "What would this babbler say?" In First Corinthians 15:35 it was they who demanded to know: "How are the dead raised? With what kind of body do they come?"

There is more to be said, however. This very form of question is in the Greek language an idiom of teasing, derision, or even defiance. Paul himself resorts to the use of it in First Corinthians 1:20, retorting to his enemies with their own weapons: "Where is the wise man? Where is the scribe? Where is the debater of this age?" The Greeks had been saying that the word of the cross was foolishness. By the form of his retort Paul is replying that the wisdom of the Greeks is foolishness. More will be written on this topic in the study of First Corinthians.

55

Meanwhile let us return to the evidence, which is piling up. What more do these scoffers say? The taunting question was equivalent to a declaration that the prediction of the second coming and the destruction of unbelievers was foolishness, and the reason is given as follows: "For ever since the fathers fell asleep all things continue as they are from the beginning of creation." This means that the world is eternal and not destined to destruction and it definitely recalls the doctrine enunciated by Epicurus himself: "The universe has always been the same as it now is and always will be the same."

This declaration embodies the first two of the Twelve Elementary Principles of Physics, which Epicurus required his disciples to learn by heart: the first declares that matter is uncreatable and the second that matter is indestructible. Epicurus knew nothing of the Book of Genesis but unwittingly repudiated it. The first words of Genesis are: "In the beginning God created the heaven and earth." Epicurus had written "Of atoms and space there is no beginning, because they are eternal." Chaos was inconceivable to him, because the universe had always been an orderly cosmos.

So far, so good, but does the author of Second Peter reveal knowledge of the atoms? Beyond doubt he does and, like Paul, he calls them elements, which is a recognized synonym. Epicurus had described the atoms as hard, impenetrable, and indestructible, capable of surviving all dissolutions of compound bodies. The author of Peter's Epistle retorts that God created the world and destroyed it once with water; on the occasion of the second coming he will destroy it with fire and, verse 10, "the elements will be dissolved with fire." He even chooses to repeat himself in verse 12, "the elements will melt with fire."

The scorn of the writer for the Epicurean theory of the eternity of the universe may be better appreciated if an ancient error of translation be corrected, which still appears in the Revised Standard: "the heavens will pass away with a loud noise." Unluckily for this version the sound denoted by the Greek word may be written "Psst!" or "Pfft!" This means that so great is the power of God that this universe, which the Epicureans declare to be eternal, will be blotted out at the word of God with the sound as of a squib.

If now we pause to reflect upon the findings of these recent pages, it must become manifest what a turmoil of feeling the name of Epicurus was capable of arousing in the mind of Paul. If Luke knew that the disciples of Christ were first called Christians in Antioch, then Paul would also have known it; and if this name was coined for them to distinguish them from the disciples of Epicurus, then he must have been aware that to the populace of Antioch and to others who adopted the new names a particular rivalry was recognized between the sect of Epicurus and the followers of Christ, and by virtue of this fact Epicurus had become a sort of Antichrist. Moreover, the name of Epicurus must certainly have shot into the mind of Paul whenever he recalled the violence practiced upon his race by the notorious Antiochus, the generous patron of Epicureanism.

In the progress of this study we shall in due time discover other reasons for the conflicting emotions of Paul and in particular the attractiveness of the Epicurean ethic as opposed to its shocking theology.

# IV

# GALATIANS

## The Weak and Beggarly Elements

Iｆ ｗｅ study the writings of Paul with the proper clues and evidences in our minds, we shall find him in certain passages reasoning after the fashion of the Jews and in others after the fashion of the Greeks, and for the most part after the manner of Epicurus. When he reasons like a Jew, he is less appealing and less convincing.

In this Epistle to the fickle Galatians, for example, he forges a chain of arguments to convince the members of the church of their spiritual sonship in Abraham. If, however, it was necessary for the Galatians to become conscious of this sonship, a like necessity should exist in the religious experience of the modern Christian, but this is not true, nor can any reasoning make it seem to be true. Thus the whole argument becomes gratuitous and for that reason devoid of interest to all except a few professional scholars.

In the last two of the six chapters, on the contrary, Paul begins to reason like a Greek and an Epicurean and the interest of the modern reader is pricked and his attention challenged. These two chapters possess also a merited preference as devotional readings.

In spite, however, of this difference, the previous four chapters contain precious items of evidence for our present studies of Paul's thought.

For instance, verse 4:3, which is rendered in the Revised Standard, "So with us; when we were children, we were slaves to the elemental spirits of the universe," may be more rightly interpreted to mean: "when we were juveniles, we were slaves to the elements of the universe." The inference is that the Galatians, before they became Christians, had been Epicureans and believers in the atomic theory. The word *elements* is a synonym for *atoms*.

There is evidence also that the fickle Galatians were backsliding and reverting to the creed of Epicurus, as in verse 4:9: "how can you turn back to the weak and beggarly elemental spirits," which should be rendered "weak and beggarly elements," meaning the despised atoms.

Again, when Paul writes in the verse following: "You observe days, and months, and seasons, and years," these words can be explained in terms of the last will and testament of Epicurus. In this document, which is extant, the philosopher enjoins upon his followers the regular observances of a number of festivals, ceremonies, and anniversaries.

In the two closing chapters it will not be surprising to discover items of Epicurean doctrine, because it is in the concluding exhortations of Paul that we customarily find them. Kindly admonition was a specialty of the friendly sect and Paul's partiality for it is first-rate evidence of his knowledge of its source.

Details of this topic of admonition will be furnished in due course as this outline of the Epistle is amplified. In the meantime two items may be cited: first, the concept of freedom, as in 5:1, "For freedom Christ has set us free," which was taken over from Greek philosophy to become a blessed idea in the Christian experience; and second, the Epicurean scheme of instruction which opposes "the vice to the corresponding virtue." This was adopted and adapted by Paul; the vices become "the desires of the flesh" and the virtues become "the desires of the Spirit."

## Epicureanism in Asia

The assumption that great numbers of the Galatians had been converted to Epicureanism is quite consistent with our knowledge of the creed. It was from its very inception a missionary philosophy and equipped with a self-propagating principle. Its members were famous for their persuasiveness — "beguiling speech," as one version styles it — and upon them all was laid the injunction, "omit no opportunity to disseminate the sayings of the true philosophy." Moreover, the creed flourished especially in the middle levels of society, the bourgeois class, who were engaged in trade, so that wherever merchants fared the doctrines would be disseminated. It was abundantly furnished with handbooks for every need and no tutors were necessary.

If the upper classes in some parts of Galatia were barbarians to the Greeks, even this fact is no obstacle to believing them to have become

Epicureans. Cicero, writing a century before the time of Paul, represents one of his speakers in a dialogue as saying of Epicurus, not without a touch of scorn: "Illustrious philosopher, who caused a sensation not only in Greece and Italy but also in the whole barbarian world."

This information will gain force by amplification. Asia Minor was the only country with barbaric inhabitants that Cicero knew at first hand. As a young man he had visited the coastal cities and in his middle age he had been governor of Cilicia, the native land of Paul. Yet this is not the whole story; for many years he enjoyed the status of friend, patron, guest, and host of Deiotarus, king of Galatia, and a speech delivered on his behalf is still extant. It is consequently highly probable that his testimony concerning the popularity of Epicureanism among barbarians had been in large part derived from information gleaned from this king Deiotarus, who was a man of superior intelligence and abilities.

Neither should it be cause for hesitation that the cities of Galatia were not notable for their number, size, or importance, the prevailing economy being agricultural and tending toward large estates. When the biographer wrote of "the friends of Epicurus," for by this title his disciples were known, "so many in multitude as not to be counted by whole cities," his meaning was that the creed was flourishing also in villages and country districts, which was possible for the reason that dissemination was from individual to individual and family to family and not by schools and tutors.

To this it may be added that Epicurus himself had written "the wise man will love country life" and the Epicurean Philodemus of Gadara published a handbook, still extant in fragments, entitled *On the Management of an Estate,* in which he advised the prospective purchaser of a country property to make sure that he should have Epicurean neighbors, for the sake of good companionship. He was taking it for granted that this was possible.

It is also to the point to bear in mind that Galatia was closer to sources of Epicureanism than it was at a later time to the sources of Christianity. If the creed had invaded the country from the north, this would have been from Lampsacus on the Hellespont, where Epicurus had resided and taught for upwards of four years, 310–306 B.C., and left a flourishing school. One of his letters, the forerunners of the Epistles of Paul, was entitled *To the Friends in Lampsacus.*

It must have been from this center that the friendly philosophy extended itself along the string of cities bordering the Black Sea. One of these was Amastris in Bithynia, the population of which in the time of Marcus Aurelius was excommunicated from the use of an oracle of Apollo because the citizens were disciples of Epicurus and ridiculed prophecy. It is an interesting detail of this story that the impostor who managed the oracle complained of the Epicureans overrunning the country.

There is, however, an item of evidence about Epicureanism in those parts that is dated three centuries earlier. Shortly before 90 B.C. a brilliant disciple of Epicurus known as Asclepiades emigrated from Prusa, close to the borders of Galatia, and established himself in Rome, where he practiced medicine for fifty years, becoming the outstanding physician of the century.

If all these items be added together we may the better understand Paul's decision against entering Bithynia, as recorded in Acts 16:7. The reason there given is the veto of the Spirit of Jesus, which need not discourage us from speculating concerning the reason for the veto itself.

The condition most favorable to Paul's ministry at this stage of his activity would have been the presence of Jewish residents, the existence of synagogues, and a colony of Christian converts, because it was his custom to speak in the synagogues and it was his special talent to develop and confirm an existent church. When, therefore, we read that Paul and his companions "attempted to go into Bithynia, but the Spirit of Jesus did not allow them," we shall be guilty of no irreverence if this be taken to mean: "They explored the advisability of going into Bithynia and found out by inquiry that the Epicureans were strong and no friends were known with whom they could find lodging and hospitality."

This inference seems justified by the call to which Paul subsequently hearkened: "Come over into Macedonia and help us." It must have been the lack of such a call that deterred the party from entering Bithynia.

It will be worth our while to observe how admirably Epicureanism was equipped for the penetration of Asia. As mentioned already, the branch school at Lampsacus was strategically situated for the dissemination of the creed along the coast of the Black Sea.

On the west coast of Asia there was another school at Mytilene, opposite the Roman province of Asia, from which, according to Acts 16:6, Paul was forbidden by the Holy Spirit. Still further to the south was the original school at Colophon, close to Ephesus. Both of these schools were excellently situated for the extension of the creed to the eastward, including Galatia, because the roads leading inland from the coastal cities were numerous.

As for the southern parts of Asia Minor, if we try to conjure up a synoptic view, we shall see Christianity at a later time disseminating itself northward through Tarsus into the hinterlands, of which Galatia was one. Tarsus was in Cilicia and Paul in this Epistle to the Galatians, 1:21 and 2:1, informs us that he spent fourteen years in the regions of Cilicia and Syria.

This gateway to Asia, however, had been open to the creed of Epicurus for three centuries before Paul's time and Tarsus was a center of Epicureanism. In the second century B.C. a renegade Epicurean had made himself a tyrant of the city and ruled it for a time. In the same century a famous Epicurean philosopher named Diogenes had flourished there; his writings on the doctrines of Epicurus were in circulation for centuries. Meanwhile, Epicureanism was the court philosophy at Antioch during the reigns of at least two kings of Syria, Antiochus Epiphanes and Demetrius Soter.

Thus the same metropolitan centers from which Christianity was disseminated in the first century had been centers of dissemination for Epicureanism during the previous three centuries; and the dusty highways which radiated from these centers had been traversed by the friends of Epicurus with the handbooks of the master in their wallets long before the ardent company of Paul came plodding along those same routes on their hired mules.

At this point a plea for suspension of judgment is in order. Whether these novel interpretations of ours will meet with acceptance or not should not depend exclusively upon the degree of finality with which each particular one can be justified, but rather upon the aggregate probability with which the influence of Epicurus upon Paul can be established. The part will not stand or fall by itself but with the whole.

For instance, in this Epistle 4:3 the words "when we were children" will be interpreted to mean "when we were at the foolish age of adolescence," and in the same way we shall explain the words "when I was a child" in First Corinthians 13:11. Not only will the explanation of the former stand or fall with the explanation of the latter; the explanation of both will stand or fall with the acceptability of a complex of Pauline thought of which they will be demonstrated to form a part.

One personal trait of Epicurus that qualified him to blaze the way for Paul was his eagerness to retain the loyalty of his followers. The charm of his personality was undeniable; his teachings were compared to the voices of the Sirens and on the occasion of one of his lectures a listener was so overcome as to throw himself at the master's feet and reverence him as if a god. Yet this natural capacity was carefully supplemented by diligent planning; the loyalty of colonies of disciples in the three cities where he had taught before settling in Athens was fostered by epistles addressed to the community, by private letters, and in some instances by visits.

In Athens itself defection from his school was so rare as to become a matter of record when it did occur. So many, on the contrary, were the desertions to his Garden from other schools that a disgruntled Platonist was inspired to author the sour epigram: "A man can become a eunuch but a eunuch cannot become a man."

## When We Were Children

Just as Epicurus was eager to retain the loyalty of his disciples, so Paul in this Epistle shows himself vitally concerned to maintain the integrity of the Galatian church. He reveals indignation and no small consternation that his own authority has been attacked, that the party of the circumcision has been unsettling the faith of his converts and that some have become backsliders.

This high concern for the integrity of the church evokes an extended chain of argument, of the casuistic sort that Paul must have learned at the feet of Gamaliel. This will have no bearing on the present inquiry until it reaches the point where a neat and threefold analogy has been built up: first, the age before faith, when man was still under the law; second, the minority of the individual under civil law, before he becomes master of his inheritance; and third, the mental minority of the individual, before he arrives at adult competence in judgment.

The first two of the three items call for no comment; the third requires immediate amplification. The crucial words occur in 4:3: "So with us; when we were children, we were slaves to the elemental spirits of the universe." To clear away first a matter of minor importance, the word *slaves* need not be pressed. In Greek philosophy to possess the truth was styled freedom, not to possess it was slavery; thus *slave* meant virtually "heretic"; it was a term of depreciation and reproach.

The word *children* is more important. The Greek word so translated is equivalent to our English "infant," which in law may be applied to any person short of legal age. It has, however, a number of connotations, and it is one of these and not its legal denotation that applies here. It refers to persons still in their mental minority, adolescent lads whose language and thinking are not as yet characterized by responsibility. This same aspect of the age of adolescence is in Paul's mind when he writes in First Corinthians 13:11: "When I was a child, I spoke as a child," and the rest.

Most important of all are the words "elemental spirits of the universe." In the Greek text there is nothing to call for the word *spirits*. The justification for this has been dug out of an apocryphal source and makes excessive demands upon our credulity. It presumes that Paul is assuming that a curious item of superstition which was not a matter of common belief even among the Jews was a matter of common knowledge among the Galatians, who were in large part of Gallic origin.

It will consequently be much more reasonable to follow the King James Version and translate it "elements of the world," which may readily be interpreted to mean the atoms of Epicurus, as understood in his well-known principle: "The universe consists of atoms and space." The sole change in translation will be slight, to read "elements of the universe" in place of "elements of the world."

If to accept this view shall merely seem to be imposing a different strain upon our credulity, this difficulty can be gradually diminished and at length resolved by a judicious survey of the facts. An inveterate but unfortunate tradition of learning has deflected all interest away from Epicurus and all but abolished him from our accountings of ancient thought, the thought of the New Testament included. We have been habituated to acquiesce in an excessive emphasis upon Platonism and Stoicism, creeds of the few, and an excessive disregard for Epicureanism, the creed of ancient multitudes, even barbarians. If only we can habituate ourselves to correct the balance, we shall achieve a momentous increase of understanding.

Naturally, this correction cannot be made quickly. A view that is unfamiliar and unwelcome will be changed only by degrees. We must submit to allowing the evidences to accumulate and suspend a final verdict until we can view them in the aggregate.

## The Weak and Beggarly Elements

In this instance we have a bevy of evidences in brief space. It is quite in Paul's manner, having broached an idea, to return to it after an interval for amplification. Thus we first meet with "the elements of the universe" in 4:3 and find second mention of them in 4:8 in different words: "In those days, when you did not know God, you were in bondage to things that by nature are not gods." The Revised Standard reads "to beings," in order to be consistent with the reference to the mysterious "elemental spirits of the universe," which we met in verse 3 above.

There is nothing in the Greek original, however, to call for "beings" any more than "spirits." To adopt these words results in mere mystification. If we assume that "the elements of the universe" are the atoms and that it is these that "by nature are not gods," we have clarity. The Epicureans ridiculed the idea of the resurrection and the whole Pauline theology. Paul is replying to ridicule with ridicule. He is hinting at the fact, universally known in his day, that the whole Epicurean structure of thought was based upon the atom, which in his grimly satirical interpretation is made to mean that all who accepted this account of things were in bondage to mere specks of matter.

This satire is promptly rendered manifest in verse 9: "how can you turn back again to the weak and beggarly elements, whose slaves you wish to be once more?" Why "weak and beggarly"? The answer is not difficult. The belief was inherent in Judaism from the first that God was to the individual a source of strength. In Paul's theology this strength is channeled to the believer through the resurrected Christ by means of the Spirit of God; in Paul's own words, First Corinthians 15:45, "the last Adam became a life-giving spirit," that is, a source of energy for the believer. It is in opposition to this notion that the atoms are despised as "weak and beggarly." It is possible that these synonyms were deliberately chosen; the atoms are "weak" in satirical contrast with the power of God; they are "beggarly" in satirical contrast to the richness of God's grace.

Incidentally, it is doubtful whether the clash between science and

65

religion were ever more neatly presented than here. Epicurus, representing science, finds the eternal in the atom, by the incessant motion of which all things are created aimlessly, though within the limitations of natural laws. As for history, it is the evolution of the unintended. Paul, representing religion, finds the eternal in God and by his power and intelligence all things were created and continued to be providentially governed.

## Days, and Months, and Seasons, and Years

The next item in this paragraph of reproach to the backsliding Galatians runs as follows, 4:10: "You observe days, and months, and seasons, and years."

A more illuminating reference to Epicureanism could not be desired. It exhibits two aspects of interest and importance: first, it is amply explained by a section from the extant will and testament of Epicurus; and second, it anticipates the shape of things to come.

Epicurus was hardly less concerned to maintain the integrity and perpetuity of the sect he had founded than was Paul to do the same for the Christian church. To this end he ordained in his will that funds be set apart for funeral offerings for his parents and brothers, for commemorative services at regular intervals for the same and for himself and two close associates, Metrodorus and Polyaenus, who had predeceased him.

Most important, however, was the provision for monthly meetings of the sect, at which a meal was served and certain rites performed in memory of Epicurus himself and his beloved disciple Metrodorus. This commemorative meeting took place on the twentieth of the lunar month, which to Greeks in general was a holy day, a sort of sabbath, and because of its sacred character Epicurus chose it for this celebration in place of his own birthday. It must be remembered that he did not consider the gods to be indifferent to human piety, even though they were indifferent to human wickedness, and he desired to maintain for his disciples a link of reverence with the divine. In other words, these commemorative monthly meetings, to which Paul refers scornfully in the words, "You observe days, and months," were planned to possess a religious character.

This item of information need not be thought recondite. So notorious were these meetings on the twentieth that disciples of Epicurus were derisively called "Twentyers," and references to the fact are extant in Greek and Latin literature over the space of five centuries.

As for the shape of things to come, the testamentary injunction of Epicurus to perpetuate the rites "in remembrance of myself and Metrodorus" can hardly fail to remind us of the saying recorded with certainty only by Paul in First Corinthians 11:24: "Do this in remembrance of me." It is also well to recall in this connection that the savior sentiment in Paul's time was enjoying an almost universal vogue and the title of savior had been claimed for Epicurus, that his disciples spoke of following "in his footsteps" and of living "as if Epicurus were looking on," and that they took a pledge: "We will be obedient to Epicurus, according to whom we have made it our choice to live."

There is something more to be said. Epicurus himself had instituted the custom of writing affectionate memoirs of faithful disciples who had predeceased him. This custom was continued by his successors and such writings may well be thought to prefigure the Acts of the Apostles and the Lives of the Saints at a later date. Moreover, the injunction of Epicurus to commemorate the day of his colleague Polyaenus may well suggest the celebration of Saints' days in the Christian church. In point of fact, if we may venture to generalize, Paul's reproachful sentence, "You observe days, and months, and seasons, and years," may well be taken as a preview of the Christian calendar of today.

If, then, our inference is sympathetically entertained, that Paul is describing Epicurean practices, the second and larger inference will be justified, that Epicureanism anticipated the practices of Christianity and functioned as a bridge of transition from Greek philosophy to the Christian religion.

## Freedom

In this Epistle to the Galatians Paul finds it fitting to his argument to dwell somewhat on the subject of freedom, and it will be rewarding to scrutinize his treatment of it. The approach may best be made by way of a brief detour.

Paul often employs the pronoun in the plural, using "we" to denote himself, and when he writes in 4:3, "So with us; when we were children, we were slaves to the elements of the universe," we are taking him to mean: "So also with myself; when I was at the irresponsible age of adolescence, I was addicted to belief in the atoms." In other words, he pleads for the sympathy of the Galatians because, before his own conversion, he had shared their error in yielding his allegiance to the creed of Epicurus.

The fickle Galatians, however, had become backsliders and Paul is consequently moved to lament in 4:11: "I fear that I may have labored over you in vain." In the next verse he turns to exhortation, which in the Revised Standard is made to read: "Brethren, I beseech you, become as I am, for I also have become as you are." These words are simple but the meaning very obscure. The obscurity may perhaps be resolved by a keen glance at the facts as implied. Both Paul and the Galatians had once yielded allegiance to Epicurus; both had transferred their allegiance to Christ, but the Galatians had become backsliders and Paul had not. Therefore Paul writes: "Brethren, I beseech you, be like me, because I too, like yourselves, was once in error." He is exhorting them to emulate his steadfastness, just as they had once shared his error.

Here we choose a small clue, which may be worth following up. In 4:15 the Revised Standard reads: "What has become of the satisfaction you felt?" This is possibly a mere modernization of the King James translation: "Where is then the blessedness ye spake of?" Both teams of translators were working in the dark. The Greek word which is here rendered as "satisfaction" or "blessedness" is *makarismos*, and this was taken from the vocabulary of Epicurus. In this vocabulary of Epicurus it is easy to discern precisely what a word means, which is less true of the terminology of Paul because he so often presumes a fund of common knowledge in his readers which we no longer possess.

To Epicurus this word signified the joy, the pleasure without alloy, that ensues upon arrival at the truth. One of his sayings may be opportunely quoted: "Love goes dancing around the whole earth, veritably shouting to us all to awake to the blessedness of the happy life." It was a conceit of Epicurus that the individual who was ignorant of the truth was living in a sort of coma. It may consequently be more than sheer coincidence that Paul writes in First Corinthians 15:34, "Awake to righteousness," and in Ephesians 5:14, "Awake, thou that sleepest." The stock of ideas that is common to both may well arouse our curiosity and challenge our attention.

To return to our verse, 4:15: if the Greek word employed by Epicurus to denote the joy of arriving at the truth has been taken over by

Paul to denote the joy of discovering the truth as revealed in Jesus the Christ, we may translate: "What, then, has become of the joy you once experienced?"

If this interpretation marks a gain in precision, it is still not the end. We can do better. Paul is very tenacious of his topic and in this instance his mind is still intent upon the joy of discovering the truth as revealed in Christ when he writes in 5:1: "For freedom Christ has set us free." To this he returns again in verse 13: "For you were called to freedom, brethren."

This is not a change of topic. It is an amplification of the nature of the joy that ensues upon arrival at the truth. This joy is a new sense of freedom. It is remarkable in the New Testament how frequently the words *free* and *freedom* are mentioned without definition. Paul makes no attempt to define *freedom* in the passage before us. He feels no need to define it because in the Greek philosophy of the time it had already been exalted to the status of a blessed word. Greek philosophy was offering the boon of freedom to the individual, nor could Christianity, if it was to compete successfully with philosophy, omit to offer the same boon.

The word *freedom* first arrived at the status of blessedness in the political sphere as a sequel to the Persian invasion of Greece. When Persia was conquered at last by Alexander and Greece was stranded in a backwash by the march of change, the philosophers began to ponder the meaning of freedom for the inner life. After some fumbling by others it reached definition in the keen and practical mind of Epicurus. To him it became freedom from fear, freedom from all the things that the Greeks had feared: fate, fortune, physical causation, gods, death, and punishment in the afterlife. For this freedom from disturbing fears Epicurus used the word *ataraxy* or synonyms — for he was partial to synonyms — such as "calm" or "tranquillity of mind," a metaphor taken from the sea.

This transfer of the concept of freedom from the political to the inner life of man was paralleled among the Jews by a progressive increase of ethical inwardness in the religious life. Jehovah became less and less the God of Israel and more and more the God of the individual.

It was the destiny of these two parallel drifts to coalesce at last in the teachings of Jesus and still more in those of Paul. The word *ataraxy* was rejected but its significance, "calm" or "tranquillity of mind," was taken over by the word *peace*. The peace of Epicurus becomes the peace of God, built into a new structure of doctrine. The name of freedom, which stemmed from the Greek side, survived as a synonym for peace; as such it signifies freedom from all disturbing thoughts and emotions.

This is one particular in which the teachings of Epicurus functioned as a bridge of transition from philosophy to religion; part of the common ground between them was the increasing interest in the individual man and the inner life.

## The Works of the Flesh

Although the Epistle to the Galatians differs from others by its abrupt beginning, it conforms to the pattern by ending up with an admirable passage of exhortation and admonition. Exhortations to the study of philosophy were so much in vogue among the Greeks as to constitute a separate branch of writing, known as protreptic; most of the philosophers from Aristotle onward published writings under this title. Philosophy was extolled as "the guide of life," an aspiration that survives to this day in the Phi Beta Kappa Fraternity, the Greek letters of this name being the initials of the words with the meaning quoted above.

Exhortation, it must be admitted, presumes a certain amount of admonition but it was exclusively the merit of Epicurus to have elaborated this practical adjunct to exhortation. The term *protreptic* became technical in meaning quite apart from his teachings but the words *admonish* and *admonition* acquired particular meanings only within his writings and the studies by disciples of his who amplified his views. He differed from his predecessors in being a natural pragmatist, impatient of knowledge that possessed no bearing upon conduct. He was not content, for example, to draw up lists of virtues and vices and classify them as Aristotle did, after the same fashion that he classified plants and animals.

Epicurus thought of the individual as a free agent, completely at liberty to choose good or evil. Freedom, from this point of view, was liberty of choice. This point of departure was not peculiar to him, because it was inherent in ethical thought before him. The elaboration of it, on the contrary, was absolutely his own. One of his writings that became a classic was entitled *On Choices and Avoidances*. This may sound stilted to us, because it exhibits a pattern of thought that is no longer in vogue, but in Paul's time it was universally familiar among intelligent people. Traces of it in the New Testament are frequent; it is explicit in Third John 11: "Beloved, do not imitate evil but imitate good."

The teachings of Epicurus, however, were being constantly amplified and modified for the changing demand and in Paul's time there was in circulation a standard work by Philodemus of Gadara entitled *On Vices and the Corresponding Virtues,* of which one book is still extant in fragments. Paul was certainly familiar with it, and in this Epistle as elsewhere, he adopts and adapts its contents to his own needs. In adapting it he even follows his model in citing the vices before the virtues: the former become "the works of the flesh" and the latter "the works of the Spirit."

That he is adapting, not copying, is plain also from his lists. For example, the vices, as they appear in the euphemistic revision of the Revised Standard, are as follows: immorality, impurity, licentiousness, idolatry, sorcery, enmity, strife, jealousy, anger, selfishness, dissension, party spirit, envy, drunkenness, carousing; the virtues are love, joy, peace, patience, kindness, goodness, faithfulness, gentleness, self-control. If these lists be scrutinized, it will be found impossible to match each vice by a virtue; the lists are unequal in number. The opposition is between vices as a class and virtues as a class.

## False Opinions

Incidentally, the translation of the words in these lists would bear careful study in the light of our knowledge of Epicureanism but this would be tedious. A more immediate reward may be gleaned by scrutinizing Galatians 5:25, which in the Revised Standard reads in part: "Let us have no self-conceit, no provoking of one another, no envy of one another." The word here rendered "self-conceit" may be shown to have signified to Epicurus the entertainment of what he called "false opinions"; for example, the belief that wealth, fame, or power could result in happiness. On this topic he had much to say, but a single dictum may serve for illustration: "Neither is the turmoil of the soul dispelled nor any worthwhile happiness begotten either by possession of the greatest wealth or by honor and glamor in public life or by any other of the boundless ambitions of men."

71

In the present instance the "false opinion" consists in thinking that getting ahead of one's neighbors means an increase of happiness. In modern parlance this is a matter of false values. Hence we may translate: "Let us not be misled by false ambitions, provoking one another to competition, envying one another."

What Epicurus thought of envy is on record: "We should envy no man, for good men do not deserve envy and, as for evil men, the more they prosper the more they spoil their own chance of happiness." On the evil of competition his teaching may be found in an Authorized Doctrine: "The man who discerns the narrow limits of life's needs will understand how easy it is to procure what removes the discomfort arising from want, so that he feels no necessity of engaging in activities that involve competition."

The Epicurean term which translators have been wrongly rendering as "vainglory" or "conceit" or "self-conceit" is employed twice by Paul and by no others in the New Testament. The other example occurs in Philippians 2:3–4, where the Revised Standard goes far astray: "Do nothing from selfishness or conceit, but in humility count others better than yourselves. Let each of you look not only to his own interests, but also to the interests of others."

Here the principle of "the vice and the corresponding virtue" is invoked again, because this was for Paul a standard pattern of thought. The virtue is brotherly love, which cooperates; the vice is the spirit of competition, sparked by envy, the false idea that getting ahead of the other will add to one's happiness. Hence we may venture to translate: "Doing nothing in a spirit of competition or false ambition but in humility counting others more important than yourselves, every one of you having an eye not to his own advantage, but rather to the good of others."

If the findings of this chapter have seemed plausible in detail and convincing in the aggregate, then we may safely infer that Paul was assuming a knowledge of Epicurean doctrines in the minds of his readers; and so by diligent reference to the extant writings of Epicurus we may often arrive at a precision never before attained in deciphering the meanings that Paul often felt justified in expressing somewhat elliptically.

# ❖ V ❖

# COLOSSIANS

## Beguiling Speech

THE brief Epistle to the Colossians exhibits a singular neatness. It begins with a sympathetic introduction, passes over to warning and remonstrance, and concludes with friendly admonition and exhortation. This conforms to the rhetorical rule that the first and last parts of a composition should be agreeable to the hearer or reader.

The letter abounds also in evidences of Paul's concern with Epicureanism: some ten items of Epicurus' teachings are identifiable. Some of these were repellent and could only be rejected. One was in part acceptable but in the main offensive. Others were so attractive as to justify adoption. Needless to say, in no instance could the rival creed be conceded the honor of mention by name. In one verse, however, it is accorded the compliment of being referred to as philosophy (2:8), the sole occurrence of the word in the New Testament.

Foremost among the doctrines mentioned is the atomic theory of the composition of matter. This was not odious in itself; it is quite possible that Paul accepted it, just as it was accepted in Second Peter 3:10 and 12 by the author of that Epistle. In order to accept it the only necessity was to assume that God had created the atoms and could destroy them. The odious thing about the atomic theory was the use to which Epicurus had put it, claiming to deduce from it his system of knowledge, ethics and theology included. Paul's revolt against this claim is registered for us in his assertion that "all the treasures of wisdom and knowledge" are hidden in Jesus Christ or in God. Philosophy stimulated the growth of religion by the force of repulsion.

A particular feature of atomism that rendered it odious to Paul was its association with the denial of divine providence. Hence he damns it

73

(2:8) as "according to the tradition of men" and "not according to Christ." It deserves to be pointed out, however, that even this association is not inherent in the theory itself. It did not discourage Pierre Gassendi, for example, the Roman Catholic priest who sponsored the revival of Epicureanism in the seventeenth century, from accepting the theory.

The offense was not in the atoms but in the assumption of Epicurus that their motions were the primal cause of all things in a universe self-regulated by natural laws. There were gods, he taught, but no participation was assigned to them either in the government of the universe or the affairs of mankind. This teaching precluded the idea of either a general or a special providence. It precluded equally all notion of revealed religion; hence it was "the tradition of men."

Of minor rank to the items above mentioned, though not unimportant, is the warning against Epicurean ridicule of the worship of angels (2:18). A correct interpretation of the verse in question will call for a change in the Revised Standard Version, as will be shown in due time.

Midway between offensive and acceptable doctrines was one in part commendable, in part reprehensible. Epicurus recommended the simple life, including plainness of diet, but unluckily he also gave his approval to the occasional indulgence on the ground that the pleasure was increased by previous abstinence; he called this "condensing pleasure." It was Paul's verdict that the latter teaching canceled the merit of the other (2:23). A right understanding of this will again require a revision of the translation.

Among doctrines of major importance that were unconditionally repudiated was the canon of truth according to Epicurus, who set up the Sensations, and especially the sense of sight, as the chief criteria of truth. Paul's retort to this was to exalt spiritual insight, the gift of God, as the sole criterion of truth on the highest level of human experience. His scorn of his unnamed competitor is expressed in the words (2:18): "taking his stand on what he has seen, puffed up without justification by the mind of the flesh."

Paul's main exposition of spiritual insight as the canon or criterion of truth may be found in First Corinthians 2, and more detailed comment will be made upon it in that connection.

Entirely acceptable to Paul was the Epicurean sponsorship of personal purity and all the homely virtues that conduce to peace and har-

74

mony in family and community life. No less than two fifths of his space is devoted to these topics in this letter. As for the familiar Epicurean practice of opposing "the vices to the corresponding virtues," we have seen that this was not merely acceptable to Paul; he makes a fetish of it, elaborating upon it not only here but also in the Epistles to the Ephesians, Galatians, and Corinthians. Its presence accounts for the attractiveness of several of our most prized devotional readings.

## Colossae

This outline of topics will presently be amplified but precedence must be given to certain significant items concerning Colossae. It was the sort of community where Epicureanism flourished. When the biographer of Epicurus wrote "of his friends so many in multitude as not to be counted even by whole cities," he was thinking of such towns of moderate size. To have so spoken of metropolitan cities like Antioch and Alexandria would have been unjustified; in such centers the friendly philosophy undoubtedly did flourish but the conditions most favorable to its vogue were to be found in the smaller cities and towns. It discouraged all competitive careers.

Colossae, like Laodicea, where this Epistle was also to be circulated, lay a few miles inland from Ephesus. In the same district was Colophon, where Epicurus had been domiciled with his parents and three brothers during the decisive decade between his twentieth and thirtieth years, and it was there that he had worked out his system of philosophy to its completion.

This recital, however, does not exhaust the items of significance. Many years later, after he was firmly established as the head of a flourishing school in Athens, he made two or three journeys to these parts, a morsel of information that carries the more weight because he traveled nowhere else. While these journeys may suggest the missionary pilgrimages of Paul, the parallel is heightened when it is recalled that one of the published epistles of Epicurus was addressed *To the Friends in Asia,* which cannot but remind us of Paul's Epistle to the Ephesians.

Thus it is not unjustifiable to think of Colossae as situated in the homeland of Epicureanism. This inference receives confirmation from a singular fact: some seventy years ago the doctrines of Epicurus were discovered to have been carved on the wall of a colonnade in the market place of an obscure town named Oenoanda, situated some fifty

75

ST. PAUL AND EPICURUS

miles to the south of Colossae. This inscription is estimated to have run to the length of three hundred feet, and though done at private expense, could have been executed only with the approval of the local authorities. Thus in one and the same monument we have incontestable evidence of the vogue of Epicureanism in these parts and of the truth of the statement that the friends of Epicurus could be counted by whole cities.

## Beguiling Speech

The Epicureans were suave and persistent missionaries for their creed. One of the injunctions of the founder was "to let pass no opportunity to disseminate the sayings of the true philosophy." It was they against whom Paul warned the Philippians (3:2) as "evil workers," though a diligent student may well suspect that these words mean "mischievous busybodies."

As for their suavity, for this we have the word of St. Augustine, who, as he informs us himself, "would have awarded the palm to Epicurus but for his denial of divine providence and the judgment of merits." It was his choice to characterize the sect by three watchwords, Pleasure, Suavity, and Peace. It was this suavity or persuasiveness that was causing concern to Paul in far-off Rome when he composed this letter. So his heartening introductory messages are promptly followed by the warning words, 2:4; "I say this in order that no one may delude you with beguiling speech."

While this rendering may deserve a slight preference over the "enticing words" of the King James Version, it is hardly precise enough. If the translator scans the Greek sentence with diligence, it must become clear that Paul's fear is of the Christians' being reasoned out of their belief by some kind of logic. It will then be better to write: "I am saying this that no one may lead you astray with plausible reasoning."

In this instance it will be worth while to know that Paul is employing a procedure that was favored by Epicurus himself, who would lead off with a general statement and then proceed to amplify it by degrees. After this fashion the general warning of Paul against "plausible reasoning" in verse 4 is here amplified with suitable detail in verse 8: "See to it that no one makes a prey of you by philosophy and vain deception, according to the tradition of men, according to the elements of the universe and not according to Christ."

76

It will be enlightening to exemplify this "plausible reasoning" at once. According to Epicurus the source of all truth is to be found in the study of nature. To this scientific knowledge Paul has already opposed in verse 3 "the recognition of the mystery of God, of Christ, in whom are hid all the treasures of wisdom and knowledge." Thus the teachings of Epicurus are "according to the tradition of men and not according to Christ."

Again, Epicurus taught that every natural desire has a natural ceiling; for example, the natural ceiling of the pleasure of eating and drinking is the satisfaction of hunger and thirst. Therefore fullness of pleasure is possible. Fullness of pleasure, in turn, means fullness of life. To this Paul sets in opposition, verse 9: "For in him the whole fullness of deity dwells bodily and it is in him that you have come to fullness of life." Fullness of life, it is implied, means attainment to likeness to the divine nature.

Yet Paul, while amplifying his theme after the fashion of Epicurus, introduces his own variation and contrives to alternate warning against false doctrine with positive instruction. So in this instance he is prompted by the repudiation of atomism as a source of truth to set forth the mysteries of the new life in Christ and to expound the victory of the cross, verses 11–15.

After this timely exposition he returns with his usual tenacity of thought to details of warning. The Colossians would have been observing the Sabbath and other holy days with the usual regulations concerning food and fasting. If these observances had been part of the law of the land, the Epicureans would have been tolerant of them; but they were not requirements of law; they were merely rules of a sect and as such were a fit subject for ridicule. They would have been mocked as servile self-subjection to the fear of divine wrath, of which the Epicureans declared the divine being to be incapable. Observance was consequently foolishness.

It will be best to take up first the question of angels, because a little knowledge of Epicurean teaching will enable us for the first time to set to rights a perplexing verse in respect of which the Revised Standard has gone astray: "Let no man disqualify you, insisting upon self-abasement and the worship of angels." This is the opposite of the true meaning.

To the Epicureans the belief in angels would have been equivalent to the belief in demons, an inferior class of divine beings. The mere suggestion that such beings existed is said to have irritated them. All divine beings, according to Epicurus, lived remote from this earth of ours, indifferent to human wickedness and incapable even of surviving under terrestrial conditions. Moreover, to believe that divine beings performed the functions ascribed to angels would be to demean them. Lastly, if men believed in angels they would also fear them, while the fullness of pleasure, that is, happiness, required complete emancipation from the fear of gods.

A precise translation must then be worded to read: "Let no man willfully humiliate you, taunting you with self-abasement and the worship of angels."

The Revised Standard reads, "Let no man disqualify you." This is an error. The Greek verb does not mean to disqualify a candidate before a contest begins but to eliminate him while the contest is in progress and hence to humiliate. The Epicurean Philodemus in his treatise on Pride cites the example of a pompous singer who was stopped by the umpire in the middle of his song and ordered from the stage; this was the extremity of humiliation. To eliminate a contestant was to humiliate him. So we arrive at the version, "Let no man humiliate you."

## The Canon of Truth

Undeniable proof that the reference in the above verse is to Epicurean ridicule is afforded by the concluding phrases: "taking his stand on visions, puffed up without justification by the mind of the flesh."

Paul is retorting to ridicule with ridicule. Epicurus had rejected the divine reason extolled by Plato as the criterion of truth and in its place substituted Nature. He denied the existence of reason apart from the body. The ability to reason, he insisted, was a faculty of the mind, just as the ability to see and hear are faculties of the eyes and ears. The mind, he taught, was an organ of the body no less than the eyes and the ears. It is this teaching that Paul is scorning when he speaks of "the mind of the flesh."

In reality Paul is repeating the performance of Epicurus. He is reasoning after a similar fashion. Just as Epicurus had rejected the divine reason of Plato, so Paul is rejecting "the mind of the flesh." He substitutes for it the divine spirit, which is not innate in man but becomes resident in man through acceptance of the resurrected Christ. This is

78

a miracle of the religious experience. When once it has taken place, and only then, the individual becomes capable of discerning spiritual truths, because, as Paul writes in First Corinthians 2:14, spiritual truths are spiritually discerned. This topic of the canon of truth will be suitably amplified in the study of the chapter cited above.

Incidentally, when Paul writes "puffed up," this may be explained from the stage practice of employing inflated skins to build out the figure of an actor for a pompous role. The charge of overweening self-confidence was perpetually urged against Epicurus, who denied debt to any teacher, styled himself "self-taught," arrogated to himself the sole right to the title of wise man, and claimed to be the sole discoverer of truth.

The disciples of Epicurus continued to bear a similar reputation among adherents of rival schools, who set no limit to their abusiveness. That among the members of a numerous sect there were some who amply deserved such censures can hardly be doubted, but the ultimate basis of the charge of arrogance may be found in dogmatism. The Academy of Plato and the Lyceum of Aristotle had professed to be schools of inquiry. Epicurus, who succeeded them after a brief interval, came out flatly for dogmatism, as one of his sayings attests: "The wise man will dogmatize and will not be a doubter." He published his Authorized Doctrines and his Elementary Principles of Physics and encouraged memorization; his writings were textbooks.

That this dogmatism was in Paul's mind is plainly hinted by a word that he uses but once and no other writer uses it in the New Testament. It is found in 2:20, where the Revised Standard reads: "Why do you submit to regulations?" The King James has "ordinances." Literally, however, we should read: "Why do you submit to dogmatism?" The inference that these words serve to identify the dogmatic Epicurean is confirmed by the previous part of the sentence, which we venture to retranslate as a whole: "If with Christ you died and took leave of the elements of the world, why, as if living in the world, do you submit to dogmatism?"

It may even seem that at least some of the Colossian Christians, like the Galatians, had been subscribing to the creed of Epicurus before their conversion. At any rate, we have here in the space of three verses, 18–20, no fewer than five identifying tags of Epicureanism: "taking his stand on visions" or, literally, "what he has seen," which hints at the

Sensations as criteria of truth; "puffed up," which refers to the tradition of arrogance in the sect; "the sensuous mind," or literally and better, "the mind of the flesh," which should remind us of the teaching that the mind is an organ of the body just as the ears or the eyes; "the elements of the world" or "of the universe," which means the atoms and the creed of which they were the symbol; and lastly, "Why do you submit to dogmatism?" As we have seen, Epicurus was the first dogmatic philosopher.

## On Condensing Pleasure

Having now established beyond much doubt an Epicurean context of thought we are at last in a better position to interpret and translate the last verse of this second chapter. Since the King James rendering fails to make sense we quote only the Revised Standard; the reference is to "human precepts and doctrines": "These have indeed an appearance of wisdom in promoting rigor of devotion and self-abasement and severity to the body, but they are of no value in checking the indulgence of the flesh." This version makes sense but its correctness is debatable. A little-known doctrine of Epicurus may profitably be invoked. It involves the teaching we have mentioned earlier in this chapter, of which it was said that Paul in part approved and in part disapproved.

The topic is manifestly food and the use of it on feast days and other special occasions. Epicurus advocated the simple life, including the simple diet, but he did not demand an adherence to the latter under all circumstances. What he did demand at all times was self-control and the willingness to adapt one's self to conditions as one found them. It was of this principle that Paul wholeheartedly approved, as attested in Philippians 4:11: "For I have learned to be content with the conditions in which I find myself."

The teaching that Paul could not condone was known as "condensing pleasure." According to Epicurus this mortal life, being the only life, was the most precious possession of man, and it was the part of reason to so plan the whole life as to enjoy it to the full. Fullness of pleasure was the objective; fullness was exalted to the status of a blessed word.

It was part of the rational planning of life to practice a sort of economy of pleasure. The meaning of this may be made quite plain by modern examples. If we should indulge in a Sunday dinner every day, the pleasure would be diluted and thereby diminished and this would be a waste of pleasure. It is the moderation of the rest of the week that gives zest to the Sunday dinner. On such occasions the pleasure may be said to be "condensed," though modern usage would prefer to say "enhanced."

It was inevitable that this idea of "condensing pleasure," even if approved in practice, should have evoked scorn. The very name of pleasure is frightening to strict moralists and the mere suggestion of "condensing pleasure" was to compound the felony, as it were. A long burlesque of the doctrine is still extant from an ancient comedy and quite appropriately placed in the mouth of a cook.

The Epicureans were derisively called "Twentyers," because they celebrated a banquet regularly on the twentieth day of the lunar month, as provided for in the will of Epicurus. If we may trust the testimony of enemies, the wines and viands on these occasions were of the best. Modern Christians, by the way, will have no excuse for murmuring, because their practice coincides nicely with the teaching of Epicurus. We celebrate not only the greater occasions, such as Easter, Thanksgiving Day, and Christmas, with richer foods, but also birthdays and other anniversaries of private life.

Let us now be very circumspect in studying Paul's judgment in this matter. In the first place, he was no ascetic; he saw no merit in practicing abstinence at all times. In Philippians 4:12 he writes, if we translate the Greek literally: "At any and all times I have learned both how to eat my fill and how to go hungry." What he did condemn, it appears, was to make a deliberate practice of preparing a sumptuous meal. This deliberate indulgence, in his opinion, canceled the merit of the previous abstinence.

The final difficulty lies in the problem of retranslating verse 23, which has long been a puzzle. If we agree with the authors of the Revised Standard, the rules of abstinence "are of no value in checking the indulgence of the flesh." If we entertain instead the suggestion made above, that the rules do possess merit but this is canceled by the deliberate indulgence that follows, we may then translate: "are of no esteem at all in view of the indulgence of the flesh."

The whole verse may then be rendered somewhat differently: "These rules do indeed possess some claim to wisdom on the score of self-discipline and moderation and self-denial in respect of the body but are of no esteem at all in view of the indulgence of the flesh."

## Friendly Admonition

It has long been a fond tradition of Christian scholars that Paul was partial to Stoicism, but the closing chapters of Colossians, like those of Galatians and Ephesians, demonstrate clearly his greater affinity with the peaceful and friendly Epicureans. The motivation may be new but the virtues are the same. The structure of meanings may have been rebuilt but the good Christian will still deport himself after the fashion of a good Epicurean.

On the level of social virtues the procedure of the Epicureans may be conveniently denoted by the words *admonish* and *admonition,* which Paul takes over from them without concealment and shares with no other writers in the New Testament. It was in the school of his suave competitors that these words had been exalted to particular importance and received a certain specialization of meaning. They signified friendly suggestion and advice unmixed with blame, censure, or reprimand. Each Epicurean group was expected to be more or less independent and devoted to mutual instruction and tactful encouragement. This is precisely what Paul coveted for his nascent Christian communities, as he often makes plain, for instance, in this very Epistle to the Colossians 3:16: "as you teach and admonish one another in all wisdom."

The content of his own admonition conforms to this pattern. All of the Greek schools of philosophy had been making studies of the virtues but they parted from one another in their structures of meanings. Aristotle, for example, arranged all vices and virtues in groups of three, the virtue being the mean between two extremes, which were vices. Thus courage is the mean between recklessness and cowardice.

Epicurus, taking his beginning from the assumption of free will in man, which consists in the liberty to choose either good or evil, instituted the expedient of opposing the vice to the corresponding virtue, as amply explained already in the chapter on Galatians. Paul takes over this expedient and handles it with admirable inventiveness. In Galatians he opposes "the works of the flesh" to "the works of the Spirit" and the latter is paraphrased as "the fruit of the Spirit." Each of these categories is buttressed by formidable lists of vices and virtues.

In Colossians he exhibits the usual devotion to this useful pattern of exhortation but the vices are now designated as "what is earthly in you," and his list is with casual discernment broken in two. In verse 3:5 we should observe the vices that are personal to the individual: "immorality, impurity, passion, evil desire, and covetousness." In verse 8 we should observe those vices that directly affect the relations of the individual with others: "anger, wrath, malice, slander, and foul talk."

The corresponding virtues are handled with a similar view to variety and emphasis; the formal list is brief: "compassion, kindness, lowliness, meekness, and patience," while forgiveness and love are separated from the rest for special stress. In all this Paul was urging nothing that the Epicurean might not have stressed, but for the conclusion he singles out the motivation, which was new, verse 17: "do everything in the name of the Lord Jesus, giving thanks to God the Father through him."

A pause for reflection at this point may serve to give a lift to our understanding. Philosophy reacts upon religion through the forces of attraction and repulsion. An example of the attraction in the case of Paul is his partiality for the expedient of opposing the vice to the virtue. An example of the repulsion may be found in the motivation. To his disciples Epicurus was a savior. They were encouraged to live "as if Epicurus were looking on." They took a pledge: "We will be obedient to Epicurus, according to whom we have made it our choice to live."

Thus Epicurus, though long since in his grave, was still to a multitude of people a personal leader and, so far as Paul was concerned, a sort of Antichrist. It is for this reason that Paul remains so deeply concerned about the motivation of conduct. For the genuine Epicurean the head of the house, in a way, was Epicurus. Knowing this, we shall better appreciate what is in the mind of Paul in making a fetish of the word *head*. In this Epistle, for example, 2:10, Christ is "the head of all rule and authority" and in Ephesians 5:23 he is "the head of the church." This principle in our day, of course, has the status of a Christian dogma but in Paul's time it was an innovation, a doctrine fresh from the mint of his mind and rendered indispensable by the rival eminence of a revered philosopher.

The case is similar with the virtue of gratitude. In the verse 3:17 Paul joins the exhortation "to do everything in the name of the Lord Jesus," with a supplement, "giving thanks to God the Father through him." Epicurus had already exalted gratitude to the status of a blessed concept in the public mind by multifarious teachings. He discerned in the corresponding vice, ingratitude, an enemy of happiness and he urged gratitude to parents, teachers, friends, and even to Nature: "Thanks be to blessed Nature, because she has made the necessities of life inexpensive and expensive things unnecessary." To this it should be added, as a momentous addition, that to Epicurus himself, as the discoverer of truth, was due the supreme gratitude.

With such details of the background in mind we may the better understand why Paul is so assiduous in teaching that the supreme gratitude should be felt toward God the Father, the source of all good. In this third chapter alone he urges the giving of thanks no less than three times and once in the fourth.

This emphasis upon gratitude to God, however, need not imply Paul's failure to discern the value of this virtue as contributory to the happy life. He could not have overlooked the fact that ungrateful people are not only disagreeable but also unhappy. He may be taken to have assumed the truth of this. What he is demanding above all else is the centering of the religious life in God. He may even have appreciated a lesser known teaching of Epicurus, that actions may precede thoughts and the habit of giving thanks to God may engender a feeling of gratitude toward God. Thus with both men the virtue of gratitude is essentially the same, an ingredient of the happy life; Paul enlarges its application and builds it into a new structure of doctrine.

It will be equally enlightening to fix the attention for a moment upon the topic of peace. This was one of three words by which St. Augustine characterized the Epicureans. They commended all the homely virtues that made for peace and harmony in the household: forgiveness, forbearance, considerateness. These are the very qualities that Paul enumerates even in greater detail, not omitting the corresponding vices. When he urges wives "to be subject to your husbands" and husbands "to love your wives," this is for the sake of peace; only the motivation is changed, "as is fitting in the Lord."

It is because of this new motivation that Paul can be acquitted of inconsistency when he expresses scorn of Peace with Safety in First Thessalonians 5:3 and elsewhere urges the cult of peace with no less, and even more, assiduity than Epicurus. The peace of Epicurus was "according to the tradition of men"; it is replaced by "the peace of Christ," as in this context, and elsewhere by "the peace of God," but, by whichever name he calls it, "the peace of Epicurus" has preceded it in point of time. It was Epicurus who had first launched this term upon its way to become a blessed word.

## Paul and Metamorphosis

We shall be further assisted toward apprehending the process of transition from philosophy to religion by spotting and correcting an error of translation. In Colossians 3:10 the Revised Standard reads in part: "and have put on the new nature, which is being renewed in knowledge after the image of the creator." The error lies in the word *knowledge*. Knowledge is the state of knowing but the Greek word here employed is *epignosis,* which denotes the experience of passing from ignorance to knowledge or from the inability to understand to the ability to understand.

This point may seem subtle but Paul is capable of subtleties. He is referring to the miracle of the religious experience. Simultaneously with the acceptance of the resurrected Christ the individual is declared to be born again to possess a new kind of understanding, spiritual insight, by which spiritual truths are discerned and judged. If this idea be kept in mind, we may translate the whole verse: "having put off the nature of the former man along with his actions, and having put on the nature of the new man, which is being renewed after the image of its creator to possess a new kind of understanding."

It sometimes happens that the sauce is as good as the meat and in this instance our comment will be as spicy as the truth. When Paul speaks of "putting off" the one nature and "putting on" the new nature, he is thinking of the phenomenon of metamorphosis in creatures like the cicada, resembling the thirteen-year locusts of America, which is numerous in the eastern Mediterranean. It emerges from the ground as an ugly insect, literally "puts off" its chrysalis and "puts on" a new form, and begins a new life as a winged creature. This miracle of nature is suggested as an image of the religious experience.

The spice of our comment consists in this, that Paul is here appealing to the authority of Nature, which Epicurus extolled as the source of all truth. Paul is virtually inviting us to believe that the miracle of spiritual conversion is no less natural than the miracle of the metamorphosis of the caterpillar into the butterfly, if we may be prepared to substitute a more familiar example than the cicada. He even reminds us of a significant detail: the individual puts off the old nature "along with its actions"; he is reminding us that the habits of the caterpillar are quite different from the habits of the butterfly. Similarly, he would have us believe, the individual is born anew in Christ to possess a new kind of understanding, which will result in a new pattern of behavior.

It is worth while to add that Epicurus himself had appealed to the phenomenon of metamorphosis to illustrate a different truth. Thus Paul involves himself in the inconsistency of reasoning after the fashion of Epicurus to render understandable and acceptable a new truth that was quite incompatible with Epicurean theology.

If before taking leave of this Epistle we make the usual pause for reflection, we shall profit by recalling once more that philosophy influences religion by the forces of attraction and repulsion.

On the principle of repulsion we must learn to reason from opposite to opposite. For example, when Paul writes with scorn of "the mind of the flesh," we should accustom ourselves to be reminded of spiritual insight, the mind of the Spirit, as it were, which is independent of the flesh and acquired by gift through the grace of God. Again, when Paul asserts that "all the treasures of wisdom and knowledge" are hidden in God, we should let ourselves be reminded that he is tacitly repudiating the dogma of Epicurus that the principles of ethics are to be deduced from the study of nature, or, in other words, that Nature is the source of all truth.

The force of attraction operates less simply and directly. While the religious man feels a definite relish in being repelled by an alleged atheist and sponsor of expediency such as Epicurus, he experiences a signal embarrassment in being attracted. In consequence he will be careful not to admit his indebtedness and may even take measures to conceal it. Paul's device was to change the motivation. The members of his churches are to put aside "anger, wrath, malice, slander, and foul talk," not because they destroy the peace of the community, but because they are "earthly" or "works of the flesh" or displeasing to the Lord.

We may well, however, remain on our guard and not fall into the error of supposing the law of expediency to have been abrogated by the change of motive. If anger and malice and slander are displeasing to the Lord, it is because they demean the individual and ruin the peace of the community, just as Epicurus taught.

The attitude of Paul toward Epicureanism may perhaps be better

COLOSSIANS *Beguiling Speech*

appreciated if we call attention to the behavior of the Stoics. By the time of Marcus Aurelius they had incorporated so much of Epicureanism into their teachings that the guileless emperor in his *Meditations* is not even aware when he is voicing the precepts of the anonymous philosopher. Often only the label is Stoic. Epicurus was doomed to anonymity, as in the New Testament. The modern Christian is no more aware than was Marcus Aurelius of his invisible indebtedness to the kindly philosophy of a man whom history has treated with gross injustice.

# VI

# EPHESIANS

## The Prince of the Power of the Air

For the purpose of this study it should be remembered as we approach the Epistle to the Ephesians that the country around Ephesus was to Epicureanism what Galilee was to Christianity. The name of Epicurus has always been associated with Athens but he was thirty-five years of age when he took up residence there, and the city was chosen chiefly for its prestige as a cultural capital, from which a world philosophy could best be disseminated. No bid was made for the patronage of the Athenian public and conflicts with the authorities were avoided by confining instruction to the famous Garden, which was private property. The Athenians happened to be at the time in a persecuting mood and in the previous year, 307 B.C., had enacted the death penalty for any philosopher offering instruction in public without a license. The law was quickly repealed but the threat persisted.

Epicurus was born in Asia and even the Greek he wrote was not the pure Attic. His birthplace was the island of Samos, where he received his early and secondary education and lived to the age of eighteen. For ten years he was afterward domiciled with his parents and three brothers at Colophon, except for intervals of schooling, mainly at the neighboring Teos. These three places are all close to Ephesus and it was in this region that Epicurus wrestled with the problems of the nature of things and of human conduct; it was there he experienced his illuminations and kneaded his philosophy into a coherent whole. After becoming famous he visited the region two or three times and composed an epistle addressed *To the Friends in Asia.*

The situation is consequently unique so far as the enterprises of Epicurus and Paul are concerned. The latter had almost seemed to be avoiding the parishes of Epicurus. Had he entered Bithynia, he might have emerged on the Hellespont where his predecessor had taught for four years, but he was dissuaded by the Spirit of Jesus (Acts 16:6–7). Had he entered the Roman province of Asia, he might have emerged at the coast and visited Mytilene, where Epicurus had taught briefly and founded a colony of disciples, but he was forbidden by the Holy Spirit. Only at Ephesus, therefore, were the rival creeds of these two gifted men contending with each other on ground that was common to both.

It is tempting to make a comparison of the two. Some modern Plutarch might discern in such a project an enticing opportunity to produce a new specimen of Parallel Lives. Both men were celibates on principle, and dubious of the blessings of wedlock. Both men were afflicted by ill health and yet both were capable of more labor than robust individuals. Both had a way of picking up faithful followers: during his brief sojourn in Mytilene Epicurus picked up Hermarchus, who lived with him ever afterward and became his successor as head of the school; in like manner Paul picked up Timothy at Lystra, who shared all his subsequent labors. Both men demanded and commanded loyalty of all converts and went to all lengths to retain it. Epicurus was bent upon proclaiming to all men the call to the happy life; Paul was bent upon awakening all men to the call of the cross, even if it meant persecution. Both men were agile fencers with the rapiers of logic and both erected coherent structures of doctrine.

An amusing item of similarity between the two is the gift of persuasive speech. It is amusing because Paul warns his converts against the "enticing words" or the "beguiling speech" of the Epicureans, though possessing a like talent himself to a remarkable degree. The teachings of Epicurus were likened by his followers to the voices of the Sirens, but no more Siren-like passages need be sought in literature than the thirteenth or fifteenth chapters of First Corinthians or the concluding part of this very Epistle to the Ephesians. All three passages exhibit the persuasiveness of a man who has mastered the rules of the schools without being mastered by them, who moves toward the goal of his argument with the ease of practiced experience and carries his readers along with him to a predetermined climax and glad conviction.

## The Prince of the Power
## of the Air

There was one talent the exercise of which was denied to both Epicurus and Paul. Both were ardent moralists, a noble breed of men but as such forbidden the use of humor. The one form of wit that befitted them was satire, which belittles the competitor and lingers in the memory. Epicurus was a master of it. He dubbed the Platonists as "hangers-on of Dionysus," the god of the theater; he referred to them as "the men who pitch their voices low," as if unemployed actors, would-be Hamlets, as it were, itching for kingly roles. Paul belittled the Epicureans as a Peace-at-any-Price Party or Safety-First Party, designating them by their catchwords Peace and Safety; but his masterpiece of satire is to be found in this Epistle: he satirizes Epicurus as "prince of the power of the air."

These words have the sound of something mystical but there need be no mystery about the interpretation. The meaning may be hidden out of sight but it is not buried out of reach. If it is not manifest at a glance, this is because it is built into a structure of thought such as both Epicurus and Paul knew well how to handle. To arrive at the meaning it is necessary to analyze the structure, take it apart and put it together again. Those who are incapable of such an operation or shrink from the effort will not understand Paul's writings. His truth is not presented in pellet form, for which the reader had better go to the Book of Proverbs. Though it be true that truth is more easily ingested in the shape of a pill, the hard fact remains that the more potent and lofty truths resist reduction to such a form.

It is partly the fault of the translator and partly the fault of the reader that "the prince of the power of the air" seems mystical. The word *prince* will mislead us. The Greek word so translated is *archon*, which may be found even in a small English dictionary. It means "ruler" and is so rendered in the Gospels. It can be employed of Satan or Beelzebub and this association of ideas may mislead us. Epicurus denied belief in all demons or inferior deities and consequently it would be out of place to think of him as ruler of agents of mischief. With this caution in mind it will be well to postpone the interpretation of the word *prince* until the meaning of "the power of the air" has been discovered.

## The Power of the Air

The interpretation of this phrase involves a neat problem in semantics. The natural impulse will be to appeal to the common sense of mankind. This will suggest to us that in every language there must be a word meaning "air" which can be equated to words in other languages meaning "air." Unfortunately this is not true; it is a tragic fact of life that common sense can prevent a man from discerning the truth and has often become an obstacle to the advancement of science.

Our modern knowledge often prevents us from understanding the ancients. We know too much; we know that air is mainly a mixture of oxygen and nitrogen, which can be condensed into a liquid for many useful purposes and curious experiments. To the Greeks, on the contrary, air was the inert component of the atmosphere, and Paul's readers so understood it. It was motionless and cold; it could not be heated, though heat could be mixed with it, because heat was regarded as a separate element. Moreover, wind was not believed to be air in motion; it too was a separate element, the restless and mobile component of the atmosphere. It was the nature of wind to be in motion just as it was the nature of air not to be in motion.

From this nonsensical structure of thought, which even to Aristotle seemed to be common sense, we pass next to an Epicurean structure. To Epicurus "the power of the air" was to produce calm; by nature it was motionless and hindered motion in other elements. Atoms of air, as ingredients of the human soul, engendered tranquillity of mind and serenity of countenance. An excess of air in the soul accounted for the placidity of the ox or, as we should say, the contented cow. Similarly, an excess of wind in the soul resulted in the flightiness of the deer. An excess of atoms of heat, in turn, resulted in anger. Hot-tempered men were believed to be subject to sudden inrushes of heat which were capable of throwing them off balance and causing them to act for a time like madmen. According to Epicurus "a fit of anger is a brief spell of insanity."

This line of reasoning was employed by him to explain the diversity in human character. This diversity was inconceivably great because the variety of differences in the atoms was beyond reckoning. The important point for the present inquiry, however, is the fact that the character of a man is subject to control and the key element for purposes of control is air. It is cool by nature and motionless, hostile to heat and motion. Its preponderance in the soul produces tranquillity in the breast and serenity of countenance, which was called ataraxy. This is confused in the best English dictionaries with Stoic apathy, a grave mistake. Apathy meant immunity to all emotions, which were thought to interfere with the verdicts of reason. Epicureans, however, had no distrust of normal emotions but only of upsetting emotions, such as fears.

It follows that the secret of preserving the coveted tranquillity of soul depended upon the control of fears. If once the fears have been brought under control, the atoms of the disturbing elements, such as wind and heat, are expelled from the soul; their room is filled by the inert atoms of air and, to quote a phrase of Epicurus, "every tumult of the soul is stilled."

All of this theory, in Paul's time as commonplace as the contents of any high school textbook of physics today, was offensive enough because it was godless science and explained phenomena without divine causation; but what must have aroused Paul's scorn above all else was the teaching of Epicurus that the most upsetting of all fears were those of the gods and death. This was the implication of the two Authorized Doctrines which he placed at the head of the whole list, an eminence from which they became known to the ancient world as were perhaps no other texts.

If this exposition be now brought to a point, it can be seen that Paul, with the true instinct of a satirist, knowing that satire is often better than argument, selects from the teachings of Epicurus the particular doctrine that lent itself to ridicule. He is scorning the idea that peace of mind, the tranquillity of the Epicureans, can be brought about by atomic control and he holds Epicurus up to scorn as the champion of such control.

As is frequent in such satirical jabs, the meaning flickers between two senses; at one and the same time Paul ridicules Epicurus as the master of a creed and as the idolized master of a far-flung multitude of disciples, who so revered him even centuries after his death that disloyalty was denounced as parricide. It may not be irreverent to detect also a glimmer of jealousy, because the reader must be blind who cannot discern in Paul a greed for the very sort of dominance that Epicurus had achieved in life and had not lost in death. It is permissible, therefore, to accept the translation, "the prince of the power of the air," if it be taken as a sneer.

The correctness of the identification of Epicurus with "the prince of the power of the air" is confirmed by two phrases, the one that precedes it and the one that follows it. The former reads in the Revised Standard, "following the course of this world," but the Greek reads, "according to the generation of this world." The latter is correct and understandable; the Epicureans are "the generation of this world" because they deny the existence of any other than the physical world, and thereby deny the existence of a spiritual world such as Paul located in the heavenly regions.

The second of the two confirmatory phrases reads, "the spirit that now is at work in the sons of disobedience." The Epicureans are correctly described as "sons of disobedience" because they deny divine creationism as described in the Book of Genesis, reject the law and the prophets, and ridicule the idea of the second coming, the resurrection, and judgment. This item of designation occurs again in Ephesians 5:6, where Paul warns his readers against the persuasions of the Epicureans: "Let no one deceive you with empty words, for it is because of these things that the wrath of God comes upon the sons of disobedience." Another occurrence of the phrase may be found in Colossians 3:6 where the context helps to identify reference to the Epicureans.

As a parting touch to this topic of "the prince of the power of the air" it should be recalled how vehemently Paul insists in his letters upon the resurrected Christ as the head of the whole structure of the church. This vehemence and insistence presumes the existence of a rival and contrary program and an unnamed adversary. In this present study the contrary program is identified as Epicurean materialism and the adversary as Epicurus. This opposition was more important to Paul than the opposition of orthodox Jews, because he was the apostle to the gentiles.

## The Fullness of Christ

It is assuredly no accident that in the very last sentence of the paragraph immediately preceding the mention of "the generation of this world" and "the prince of the power of the air" Paul writes of "the fullness of him who fills all in all," and after an interval writes, in 4:13, of "the mature manhood" and "the measure of the stature of the fullness of Christ." Strange as it may seem, or even farfetched, there are consecutive steps of logical connection between the concept of air as

93

an agent of tranquillity of soul and the concept of fullness as denoting attainment to godliness. It must always be carried in mind that Epicurus and Paul have this in common, that their ideas are regularly embedded in structures of thought and not offered as isolated bits of wisdom such as we know in the Book of Proverbs.

Epicurus and Paul had also this in common, that they conceived of the individual as progressing toward an appointed goal by definite steps or degrees, a notion that was shared with the mystery religions. In this teaching the Epicureans, as the older sect, enjoyed priority; one of their original textbooks bore the title, *On the Progress toward Wisdom*. The goal, it need hardly be said, may be variously described: in the case of the Epicureans it was wisdom or fullness of pleasure or approximation to the life of the gods; in the case of Paul it was knowledge of God or saintliness or likeness to Christ or fullness of Godhead.

Now, strange as it may seem, or even startling, Paul teaches that one of these definite steps of progress toward the Christian's goal is to outgrow the belief in the philosophy of Epicurus and his atoms. In Galatians 4:3 he had written: "When we were children we were slaves to the elements of the universe," that is, the atoms, which farther along in verse 9 he scorns as "the weak and beggarly elements," as if serious truth could be built upon the contemptible atoms. In this passage the word *children*, as the context shows, signifies persons still short of mental maturity. It is just as if he were saying that belief in the atoms was excusable for adolescents but not for adults.

If now we turn back the pages to Ephesians 2:1–2, we find that to outgrow Epicureanism is to pass from the death of sin to the life of the spirit. This is analogous to the passing from the minority of the spirit to true heirship in Christ, as set forth in Galatians. The figure of speech has been changed but the structure of thought is the same: to outgrow the belief in Epicurean materialism is a definite step in the progress toward the fullness of Godhead.

It was not Paul, however, who first exalted fullness to the status of a blessed word. It must have been a thorn in his side that "the prince of the power of the air" had so often picked his words for him. At any rate he felt the necessity of giving much earnest study and thought to discovering for them new settings of significance.

It was in connection with the concept of pleasure that fullness became a blessed word. Plato had sponsored the popular opinion that

94

pleasures have no natural limit; they continually breed; the greater the indulgence the greater the need of indulgence. Epicurus, on the contrary, exalting Nature as the norm of truth, rightly called attention to the fact that natural limits had been set, the satisfaction of thirst and hunger being, for example, natural limits to the pleasure of drinking and eating. Consequently, if only a man be wise, the fullness of pleasure is possible, all natural pleasures being limited by natural ceilings.

For another reason also the fullness of pleasure was declared possible. According to Epicurus the number of pleasures is limited and "no new pleasure can be devised." Thus in a single lifetime the list of pleasures can be exhausted. Moreover, if fullness of pleasure has been once attained, he insisted, it cannot be increased by infinite time. This was part of the structure of thought by which he strove to reconcile men to mortality.

Although this may perhaps have been sufficient to exalt pleasure to the status of a blessed word and capable of exercising a warming effect upon the mind, it was not the whole argument. There was still another floor to this edifice of thought. According to Epicurus there were two kinds of pleasure, the one kind being subject to addition and subtraction, which was human, the other being perfect, which was divine and characterized the life of the gods. It follows, therefore, that in proportion as human beings by wise and rational living attain to the fullness of pleasure they approximate to the life of gods.

Moreover, on the physical side, this approximation to the life of the gods means the expulsion from the soul of all rebellious atoms, leaving a preponderance of the placid atoms of air. On this point it is worth the time to quote the text. The Epicurean poet Lucretius writes: "This assurance I seem to be able to give in these matters, that so infinitesimal are the traces of our evil natures that reason cannot expel from the hearts of the wise that nothing prevents men from passing a life worthy of the gods."

If this whole structure of thought can be apprehended and kept in mind, it becomes imperative to observe a logical sequence of thought when Paul toward the end of the first chapter of this Epistle represents Christ as exalted "above every name that is named" and in the next chapter derides Epicurus as "the prince of the power of the air." No two names were in those days so distinctly set against each other as those of Epicurus and Jesus; the very name *Epicurus* means "helper" or "succorer" in Greek and multitudes of men revered him as a savior. It was to distinguish the disciples of Jesus from the disciples of Epicurus that they were called Christians. The two sects were unique in being named for their founders.

To return to our argument, we should recognize the logic of Paul's procedure when in the first chapter he works up to a climax and caps it with the words, "the fullness of him who fills all in all," and promptly turns to the task of pulling Epicurus down from the pagan eminence.

This is not the end, however; the argument marches on. The Epistle is constructed after the manner of a Greek victory ode, approaching the theme and then receding from it as if in harmony with stirring music and the progression and recession of a chorus of dancers. In 4:13 the progression of thought arrives once more at a climax and one of loftier elevation: until we all attain "to mature manhood, to the measure of the stature of the fullness of Christ."

Incidentally, Paul works in the domain of doctrine after the same fashion as ancient architects, who tore down pagan temples in order to build Christian churches. The older structure furnished material for the new. Paul demolishes philosophy in order to build up religion.

To return once more to the argument, the scheme of thought repeats itself. Just as the name of Christ had been exalted and the name of Epicurus anonymously belittled, so now the words "mature manhood and the measure of the stature of the fullness of Christ" are immediately followed by the words "so that we may no longer be children." This is one of the three passages where the creed of Epicurus is scorned as something to capture the immature, the college boys and girls, as we may say. One passage, already cited, is in Galatians 4:3: "when we were children we were slaves to the elements of the universe," that is, "the weak and beggarly elements," the atoms. The third is in First Corinthians 13:11: "When I was a child, I spoke like a child," of which a fuller interpretation will be offered in its proper context.

The present mention of children, however, is followed by words that tempt to further inquiry: "tossed to and fro and carried about by every wind of doctrine." It is curious that Epicurus had written something very similar, and, as usual, it was part of one of his structures of thought. Since he denied immortality, it followed that the present life could not be viewed as a preparation for a finer life after death, as it was to Plato and ought to be for Christians, but was rather a preparation for a happy old age, as modern society tends to believe. Old age was thus the haven or harbor of the voyage of life.

The beautiful words of Epicurus on this topic run as follows: "It is not the young man who is to be thought happy, but rather the old man who has lived the good life; for the young man, led astray by his high spirits, *as a general thing drifts at the mercy of chance*, but the old man has cast anchor in old age as in a haven, locking in a grateful memory the recollection of blessings he had no right to count upon."

With the words in italics compare those of Paul, "tossed to and fro and carried about with every wind of doctrine." Both men are describing the age of adolescence.

This slight coincidence, it is granted, is no proof that Paul was familiar with the words of Epicurus but scores of such specimens can be assembled, and even small probabilities can add up to certainty. Paul seems to have been disposed toward Epicureanism as was the illustrious Cicero. Both of them continued to feel the pull of the enticing persuasiveness, the *suavitas*, as St. Augustine called it, which filled whole cities with disciples.

Both men also stood in fear of that very persuasiveness. It was for this reason that Cicero in his old age reverted to orthodoxy and denounced the alluring creed of the hedonistic Sirens. It was for a like reason that Paul continued to warn his converts of their "enticing words" or "beguiling speech." In this instance, Ephesians 4:14, the warning is against "the cunning of men" and "their craftiness in deceitful wiles."

It is tempting, however, to seek greater precision in the translation of these phrases. Paul by his choice of words would have us think of suave gamblers who lie in wait for the unsuspecting adolescent with loaded dice, unscrupulous as to the means of their deception.

Epicurean teachings, however, had a way of recurring to the mind of Paul. No sooner has he warned his readers against the persuasiveness of the competitor than he counsels them, 4:15: "Rather, speaking the truth in love." What this means will be more precisely understood if it be recognized as a specialty of the Epicureans. Each of their groups was a mutual education society and each member was required to submit to correction without animus. The Epicureans had their own schools, an example which the Christians copied, and in these the first objective was to habituate the child to take correction kindly. The

97

teacher was to be actuated solely by a desire to advance the good of the pupil and was warned against taking any misconduct as an affront to himself. He is warned against reviling, jeering, or injuring feelings.

On this topic we still possess in extensive fragments the Epicurean textbook, of which the title may be interpreted *On Speaking the Truth*, by Philodemus of Gadara. It may very well have been known to Paul.

How persistently the problem of combatting Epicureanism exercised the kind of Paul — it may have been his thorn in the flesh — is immediately evidenced again. No sooner has he exhorted his followers (4:15) "to grow up in every way into him who is the head, into Christ," than he turns to warning again in verse 17 (Revised Standard) against living "as the gentiles do, in the futility of their minds." The King James has "vanity" instead of "futility." The latter is preferable but greater precision is possible.

The Greek word which is so translated is one of several that do not occur in the Gospels but are used by both Paul and the Epicureans. To the latter the corresponding adjective meant "silly" or "nonsensical"; it was a word of ridicule. For example, one of the sayings of Epicurus runs: "It is silly to pray to the gods for something a man is capable of obtaining for himself." Another saying reads: "Those who say the soul is by nature incorporeal are talking nonsense."

From statements such as these, which are on record, it is easy to infer that the Epicureans had been treating the whole program of Paul's evangelism with ridicule: they would have been saying that the prediction of the second coming, the judgment, and the resurrection of the dead were all silliness. Consequently, when Paul writes of "the silliness of their minds," he is merely answering ridicule with ridicule and hurling back at his adversaries one of their own grenades. That this ridicule, however, was the cause of bitter concern to him may be discerned from First Corinthians, where "to the Greeks foolishness" or something similar is found five times.

## Nurture and Admonition

From the ethical advice and exhortation that Paul sets down for his readers verse 6:4 may be singled out for special comment: "Fathers, do not provoke your children to anger, but bring them up in the discipline and instruction of the Lord" (Revised Standard); the King James reads "nurture and admonition."

There is more here than meets the eye and, as so often in Paul's writing, what does not meet the eye may be dug up from texts of Epicurus. It will be recalled that the latter in his first Authorized Doctrine declared the divine being to be incapable of anger. To this it may be added that he held up the life of the gods as a model to be imitated, including this immunity to anger.

How Paul appropriated this doctrine, changed the motivation, and presented it as his own teaching may be observed in this Epistle 5:1–2: "Therefore be imitators of God, as beloved children. And *walk in love*, as Christ loved us and gave himself up for us." This is characteristic of Paul: he takes an idea from Greek philosophy, elaborates it, embellishes it, remotivates it, and presents it as something new.

After this brief detour it will be possible to return to "the nurture and admonition of the Lord" with better prospects of precise and fruitful interpretation. If men are to imitate the divine being, as Epicurus recommended, and to become "imitators of God," as Paul enjoins, and "walk in love," as both advised, they will neither give way to anger themselves nor by displaying anger provoke their children to anger. Like the good Epicurean teacher, they will be actuated solely by the good of the child.

As for "nurture and admonition," the key word is *admonition*, which, counting the verb *admonish*, occurs twelve times in Pauline writings and nowhere else in the New Testament. With Epicurus it is technical and signifies the gentlest sort of instruction in conduct, free from rebuke or reprimand and characterized by timely suggestion rather than sharp imperatives. It is consequently at the sacrifice of accuracy that the Revised Standard drops the word *admonition*. The accurate version would read "the instruction and admonition of the Lord."

Thus a commendable item of procedure is taken over from philosophy and transmitted to us under the label of religion. This phenomenon is not singular; various borrowings from Epicureanism were made by the Stoics and come down to us under their labels.

## This Present Darkness

Concerning other ethical precepts of this letter the place for comment will be elsewhere in this study. However, there is one remarkable verse, 6:12, which calls for immediate explanation. In the whole Epistle there is a certain alternation of movement, a reciprocation between admonition and warning, but this final example of it possesses major interest. It forms a sort of final climax. Paul usually contrives, like the Epicurean poet Lucretius, to finish each piece with a passage that is apt to find lodgment in the memory forever. The verse that here calls for interpretation reads: "For we are not contending against flesh and blood, but against the principalities, against the powers, against the world rulers of this present darkness, against the spiritual hosts of wickedness in the heavenly places."

This is one of the passages that have seemed to justify scholars in regarding Paul as a mystic. It does not follow, however, that Paul was a mystic because scholars are mystified. The real trouble may be that the key to the mystery has not been found.

The first problem is to determine the meaning of the word *principalities*. The Greek is *archai*, one of those shifty terms of which the meaning depends upon the context. To the translators of 1611 it seemed to mean "principalities" and their choice has planted a prejudice in the minds of their successors. The real question, however, is not what the word seemed to mean in 1611 but what it actually meant to readers when Paul wrote it, in the first century A.D. To readers of that time, when the lore of the atoms of Epicurus was as much a part of the public mind as the lore of atoms and atomic fission is a part of the public mind at this moment, the word would have signified atoms. The root meaning is "beginning" and the atoms were the beginnings of all things according to Epicurus.

What, then, can Paul be meaning when he declares the contest to be not against flesh and blood but against the atoms? The answer is easy: he means that the real enemy is an ideology.

It remains to discover how the remaining terms of the list will fit into this interpretation. What is meant by the second: "against the powers"? This word has been explained already, when "the prince of the power of the air" was under scrutiny. The word *power* signified the fixed potency, *finita potestas*, as Lucretius has it, which characterized each particular variety of atom, in modern chemistry the valence. For example, atoms like those of air always tended to produce tranquillity; those resembling the atoms of wind always tended to produce motion, and so on with each sort.

So this interpretation of the word *powers* is quite in harmony with the interpretation of the previous word as "atoms." There is no need to see mysticism. What should be discerned is the religionist's scorn of science and its terminology.

So far, very good, but what about "the rulers of the darkness of this world," or "the world rulers of this present darkness," according as the King James or the Revised Standard is preferred? These are everyday words but in combination they evoke no click of understanding in the mind of the modern reader. This failure is due to the obsolescence of certain reflexes of thought to which Paul's readers were conditioned and we are not.

The clue to these obsolete reflexes, however, may be found in the teachings of Epicurus, which it has long been the fashion to ignore.

In this instance the pursuit of the clue will be very rewarding, because it will bring to light a fundamental paradox of popular thought in Paul's time, which occurs not infrequently in his Epistles. This paradox hinges upon the figurative use of the words *darkness* and *light* to denote respectively states of sin and salvation. This reciprocal metaphor has become for us so staled by frequence as to deflect from itself all critical attention. It may consequently be somewhat startling to bring to notice that the Epicureans made figurative use of these same words *darkness* and *light* to denote the very opposites: religion was darkness and to be saved from religion was emergence to light. It was the boast of Epicureans that their founder had emancipated mankind from the yoke of religion.

The first book of the Epicurean poet Lucretius begins with a description of mankind "lying prostrate upon the earth, foully crushed beneath the burden of religion," and the third book apostrophizes Epicurus as "the glory of the Grecian race, who out of such profound darkness was the first to succeed in raising aloft so brilliant a torch of light that men could see what made life worth living." This light which was raised aloft, it is needless to insist, was the light of natural science, with its atoms and their powers.

Now this crisscrossing of metaphors, religion being dubbed as darkness by the one sect and exalted as light by the other, is not merely astonishing but also fruitful of consequence. It again puts Epicurus in the position of Antichrist, whom Paul never names, though he sponsors the concept.

Moreover, to advance the argument a stage farther, the effect of the teaching of Epicurus was to dethrone the gods, though not to abolish them; they were to be relegated to a retired life, as it were, free to enjoy absolute happiness, worried by no responsibility, and unconcerned about human wickedness. Thus, insofar as he dethroned the gods — and this would apply to Jehovah as soon as Epicureanism had invaded Palestine — he exalted himself above them. Hence Paul writes in Second Thessalonians 2:4: "who opposeth and exalteth himself above all that is called God," quite rightly discerning that all gods fare equally ill at the hand of Epicurus.

When once the argument has been advanced to this point, there is no longer reason to be mystified about the meaning of Ephesians 6:12, "against the world rulers of the present darkness." A brief chain argument will sum up the case: if the Epicureans would dethrone all gods, Jehovah included, and retire them to inactivity, then they exalt themselves above the gods; and if they exalt themselves above the gods, they may well be styled ironically as "world rulers" themselves. Epicurus himself, as the principal, may well be described as "the man of lawlessness" and his disciples as "the sons of disobedience." Would they not have abolished the Ten Commandments along with the rest of the law? If for the law and the prophets are to be substituted the writings of Epicurus, including his forty Authorized Doctrines, then as lawmakers as well as usurpers the Epicureans would have qualified themselves for the derisive epithet of "world rulers."

Paul is retorting to ridicule with a more elaborate and more devastating ridicule; he is outmocking the mockers. Words often lose their voltage in translation and this is particularly true of words of derision. The word that we feebly render as "world rulers," when read in the Greek tongue, may be felt to detonate with a veritable blast of scorn; it is a big compound noun, polysyllabic, sonorous, and contemptuous, rare at best and used only here in the New Testament. It hints at the alleged arrogance of the Epicureans.

Moreover, when Paul writes of "this darkness," it is almost as if he were putting this phrase in quotation marks; he refers to the fact that to these arrogant adversaries religion is darkness. It is even possible that it was from Paul that his faithful Luke picked up the potent idea, found only in his Gospel, 11:35: "the light that is in them is darkness."

Of four designations of the adversaries only one remains. In the King James Version it reads: "spiritual wickedness in high places." This belongs to the class of mistranslations that endear themselves to Bible readers; it is astonishing how apt a mistranslation can be to certain circumstances. The Revised Standard hints at a mystical meaning, though edging closer to the truth: "the spiritual hosts of wickedness in the heavenly places." Unluckily there is nothing in the Greek text to demand the word *hosts* and the suggestion of mysticism ought to put us on guard. Paul's references are usually specific.

This specific reference may be found in the same source from which we have drawn our solutions to the other enigmas of this compacted verse, which would have been no enigmas to contemporary readers.

A literal translation would read: "the spirituality of wickedness in the heavenly regions." It was the teaching of Epicurus that the world we live in and other worlds resembling it in the infinite universe were areas of imperfection and corruption, and that in the spaces between these worlds, not unaptly described here as "heavenly regions," was an area where perfection and incorruption prevailed. In this area was located the abode of "the blessed and incorruptible being" which Epicurus refers to in the first of his Authorized Doctrines.

To this concept of the divine being Paul could not deny all merit, because this being was represented as partial to pious and reverent human beings and as offering them a sort of fellowship; but there was something ascribed to it that horrified him: total indifference toward human wickedness. What could be more wicked than indifference toward wickedness? Hence we have this blasting figure of speech, the phrase that contradicts itself, "the spirituality of wickedness in the heavenly regions."

## The Logic of Opposites

The time has now come for the synoptic survey of this Epistle. If we would clinch our understanding of it, the procedure of reasoning from opposite to opposite should be singled out for exclusive attention. This has been mentioned already but a striking example may serve to bring our conception of it into sharper focus. When the Moslem says, "The Lord God is one God and Mohammed is his prophet," he is denying the Doctrine of the Trinity and the divinity of Jesus. In other words, unless the divinity of Jesus and the Doctrine of the Trinity had won recognition, the Moslem could never have denied them. The one religion was born of the other through the force of repulsion.

Similarly, if the philosophy of Epicurus had not flourished in advance of Christianity, then Christianity as Paul constructed it would not have existed. The form it was given by him was due to the force of opposition and repulsion. The very name of Christian was bestowed upon the disciples to distinguish them from the followers of Epicurus. The adherents of no other sects were named for their founders.

No time should be lost in fortifying this general statement by examples. When Paul insisted that Christ was the head of the church, he was endeavoring to habituate his readers to the thought that the community he was setting up was no mere school of philosophy headed by a mortal man, such as Epicurus, no matter how gifted, but a divine institution and headed by a divine man, whose exaltation to the right hand of God was an historical fact.

Next, when he proposed to exalt the name of this divine man Christ "above every name that is named," the fact that the name of the Antichrist, as it were, which was in his mind at the moment was no other than Epicurus is demonstrated by his immediate effort to depress the prestige of this Epicurus as "the prince of the power of the air," as if the happiness of mankind could depend upon paltry atoms, "weak and beggarly elements."

Recapitulation of additional examples will be justified if it serves to inculcate an unfamiliar habit of thought. When Paul writes in this Epistle of "the fullness of him who fills all in all" and "the fullness of God," he would never have so written were he not opposing this blessed concept to "the fullness of pleasure," which to Epicurus was fullness of life.

Yet again, when he describes the climax of the Christian experience as attainment "to mature manhood," he would never have been moved to choose this particular phrase had he not been insisting, as in Galatians and First Corinthians, that to accept the atomism of Epicurus was meet only for the irresponsible age of adolescence.

From the topic of repulsion to the topic of satire the transition is easy. When Epicurus, after a taste of persecution, resolved to make a weapon of ridicule, which was not an indictable offense, he became a satirist and he encouraged the practice among his followers. One of them enraged the Platonists by writing a burlesque account of Socrates. Paul too, the ex-Epicurean, identifies himself squarely with this tradition; when he dubs Epicurus "the prince of the power of the air," this is pure satire. It is pure satire also and that too with an exquisite refinement when, toward the close of this Epistle, he resorts to the ambiguous words which may be rendered "principalities and powers" but in the Greek language can just as well mean "atoms and their fixed potencies."

The Epistle is all of a piece, carefully planned, and in effect an elaborate specimen of satirical writing, interlarded with friendly exhortation and admonition, purloined from the plenteous ethical stores of the very teacher that is satirized. The forces of attraction and repulsion work simultaneously.

As a last word, it may be added that if this Epistle was really addressed to the Ephesians, we shall be moved to recall the words of the biographer of Epicurus, who speaks of his friends as being "counted by whole cities." To have composed a blistering, though not unartful or untasteful, blast of satire against a man who was not known to multitudes would be hardly conceivable.

# VII

# FIRST CORINTHIANS

## The Logic of the Cross

THE heading of this chapter has been chosen with delibera-
tion. In the light of the content of this Epistle it would seem that what
we have been accustomed to know in the King James Version as "the
preaching of the cross" and now read in the Revised Standard as
"the word of the cross," in reality means "the logic of the cross" as
opposed to what we may call "the logic of the atom."

The keynote is struck in the first chapter: Paul pours scorn upon
philosophy and in chilling irony refers to the atoms in verse 28 as
"things that are," because Epicurus asserted them to be the ultimate
existences; to these he opposes "things that are not," such as the faith,
hope, and love of the illustrious thirteenth chapter. In the second chapter he sets up the new canon of truth, spiritual insight, in direct opposition to the famous canon of Epicurus. In the fifteenth, a grand finale,
he expounds his doctrine of the soul and immortality, employing Epicurean terminology and reasonings in order to reason Epicurus out of
court.

It is well to take Paul at his word. It is in this Epistle, 9:22, that he
informs us: "I have become all things to all men that I might by all
means save some." If, then, he became "as a Greek to the Greek," we
are assuming that he became as an Epicurean to the Epicurean. The
other Greek philosophies were offering no competition. Platonism was
always for the intellectual few. Neither were the followers of Aristotle
numerous and their interest was less in human beings than in plants and
animals. Stoicism with its high pretentions attracted the "silk-cushion"
class and disqualified itself for the multitude by its asperity.

It was the ingratiating friendliness and suavity of the ubiquitous Epicureans that Paul especially feared and emulated, with which they made their neatly integrated and clearly written theories acceptable to the multitudes and especially to the middle class, the thrifty and industrious bourgeois. This suavity was defined by Cicero as "an agreeableness of speech and manners," but it also hints at persuasiveness; nor is there any Epistle of Paul that exhibits this quality to a higher degree than certain chapters of this first Epistle to the Corinthians.

Paul had received a liberal education. In this Epistle, 14:18, he writes: "I thank God that I speak in tongues more than you all." He was fortunate in the place of his birth. Tarsus was the gateway to Asia Minor from the south and in point of celebrity in the East was inferior only to Antioch and Alexandria. As part of his education the youthful Paul would have received instruction in rhetoric, as his writings amply testify. It is also likely that he was introduced to Greek philosophy by his teacher of rhetoric. It was a common procedure for the same instructor to handle both branches, devoting the morning to philosophy and the afternoon to speech. Neither was it uncommon for this instructor to be an Epicurean. It is true that the sect discouraged the political career but it is not true that they despised the arts of speech. Their devotion to the art of persuasion determined this choice in advance.

When we turn to Paul's actual procedures we must be on our guard against his beguilements. It is part of his artfulness to conceal his art. Very soon after his affectionate salutation he begins to disavow all knowledge of rhetoric and philosophy, 1:17: "For Christ did not send me to baptize but to preach the gospel, *and not with eloquent wisdom.*" As if this disavowal might fail to register itself, he repeats it presently, 2:1: "I did not come to you proclaiming the mystery of God *in lofty words or wisdom.*" As if this repetition would not suffice, he hammers upon the point with a third assertion, 2:4: "and my speech and my message were not *in plausible words of wisdom.*"

This is mere literary irony and its purpose is to forestall any impression of superiority that might diminish the acceptability of the message. In point of fact he is about to do the very things he disavows; he will be writing artfully and in this very same second chapter he will set up a canon of truth, which is a concept of sheer philosophy.

On this topic of philosophy a few more words may be helpful. Wherever Paul uses the word *wisdom* by itself he means Greek philosophy. It is one of those opposites in which his thinking abounds; it is opposed to "the wisdom of God." In verse 1:20 his scorn of it becomes explicit: "Where is the wise man? Where is the scribe? Where is the debater of this age?" This pattern of rhetorical sentence is an idiom of contempt and disparagement, as we may observe also in the question of the scoffer in Second Peter 3:4: "Where is the promise of his coming?" It is just as if Paul had written: "Of what use is the philosopher? Of what use is the man of learning? Of what use is the researcher?"

Concerning this word *researcher* a note of justification is in order. It suggests the force that the words *disputer* and *debater* of the King James and Revised Standard Versions would have carried for the ancients, whose only concept of research was a staged debate between contestants in the presence of others, after the manner of Socrates, the so-called science of dialectic. In practice this degenerated rapidly into sheer exhibitionism but continued to enjoy high popularity. To Paul it was mere "arguing about words, good for no useful end, ruinous to the hearers," as he warns in Second Timothy 2:14.

In this quotation the word *hearers* calls for a note. In the Greek language it signifies by implication "students" and thus Paul is virtually saying that "arguing about words is ruinous to students." It happens also that Epicurus long before had denounced dialecticians as "wholesale corrupters," that is, of young men. We may well accustom ourselves to finding Paul in agreement with Epicurus on many particulars even while denouncing philosophy, the "wisdom of the world," in general.

He does denounce it frequently and he wishes the members of his churches to become prejudiced against it. Yet at the very same time it is no part of his intention to reason after the fashion of a Jewish prophet, nor even, for example, as Jesus did, but rather after the manner of a Greek philosopher. He is planning to build up "the logic of the cross" into a coherent structure of doctrine to the end that the truth which in the beginning was received in faith may be confirmed by reason. This "logic of the cross" must be so presented as to rival and replace the logic of the atom.

Even on the topic of rhetoric a brief note may be in place. Paul, in spite of his disavowals of eloquence, exhibits abundant knowledge of the rules. In this Epistle we should observe, for instance, how he alternately makes sharp demands upon the attention of the reader and then

108

relaxes it. Not to press the details unduly, the first three chapters, the thirteenth, and the fifteenth call for close concentration, while in the intervals the demand for attention is somewhat relaxed; nor in this planned spacing is it to be overlooked that he takes care to end magnificently in the illustrious fifteenth, a veritable peroration. He is a practiced rhetorician.

## The Things That Are Not

If now we have penetrated the disguises of Paul and realize that he is practicing the arts of writing and reasoning as taught in the Greek schools at the very same time that he is disavowing knowledge of them, we shall be prepared to profit by a scrutiny of details.

Toward the end of the first chapter he exults that God has chosen the foolish in the world to shame the wise, the weak to shame the strong, and the low and despised, "even things that are not, to bring to nothing things that are." The key to this dark phraseology is recognition of the fact that "the things that are" in the language of Epicurus means the atoms, *ta onta* in the Greek. This is irony; according to Epicurus these atoms, apart from space, were the sole real existences; out of them all things were made and into them all things could be dissolved.

Now, if this principle be accepted, what becomes of such things as faith, hope, and love? This is an old, old problem, thoroughly threshed out in antiquity and rethrashed in modern philosophy. The answer is that such things as faith, hope, and love would be reduced to unreality, mere names, empty of meaning, corresponding to no concrete existence. The example most bandied about in ancient times was that of virtue, so much flaunted by the Stoics. For instance, the last words of Marcus Brutus became a classic; before committing suicide he is said to have lamented: "Unhappy virtue! So you were just a name, after all, and I followed thee as something real."

It matters little that this reasoning is a fallacy and that Epicurus knew the answer. If the material atom is the sole and ultimate existence, then virtue can have no existence; this inference becomes a necessity of thought. A necessity of thought, however, is not a necessity of reality, much less of action. The human mind is dominated by abstractions in spite of the fact that they cannot be contained in a test tube.

The fallacy, however, was demonstrable only to the few, while the slur was valid for the disparagement of atomism in the minds of the many, which was the objective of Paul. For the modern reader the essential thing to observe is the fact that in scorning "the things that are" Paul is scorning the atoms.

## Paul's Canon of Truth

An excellent specimen of persuasiveness joined with apt concealment of art may be observed in the second chapter of this Epistle, where Paul sets up his new canon of truth. In point of fact the concealment is so neat that even the Epicurean reader of that day may have been persuaded to accept Paul's reasoning without being aware that the canon of truth as enunciated by Epicurus himself was being replaced by one of Paul's invention. As for the modern reader, he may be in the predicament of missing the meaning entirely, because the teachings of Epicurus are no longer part of our common knowledge, nor even included in the knowledge of the learned.

As things now stand, it is much as if Paul had written in cipher and the task before us is one of decipherment. Fortunately this decipherment is quite possible and the reward will be found in clearer understanding and more precise translations.

It goes without saying that every serious thinker must possess some criterion of truth. For the majority of Greek thinkers this criterion was reason but it was something taken for granted and not spelled out in a dogma. Epicurus, the first dogmatic philosopher, took care to spell out his criterion and give it to the world in a document, a brief treatise entitled *Canon*. This word signifies in its concrete sense a rule or straightedge by which a builder tests the exactness of his work. The choice of this word should remind us that Epicurus conceived of sound thinking as an operation to be characterized by precision, analogous to exact procedures in the erection of a building. This concept is elaborated by his disciple Lucretius, who mentions also the level and plumb line.

We should also do well to remember that Paul's mind is prepossessed by a similar analogy. Witness his frequent use of the word *build* or *build up* and especially his addiction to the word *edify*, which, save for an example in Acts, he alone employs in the New Testament. By this very frequency the meaning of the word has been so washed out that few readers are prompted to recall its original significance, "to build a house," which holds true also for its Greek equivalent. Thus *edifying* means "constructive." At the moment, however, the point to bear in mind is the extent to which Paul resembles Epicurus in certain drifts of thought. This resemblance may be discerned in his elucidation of his new canon of truth.

The *Canon* of Epicurus was not only the first document of its kind but was also one of the neatest packages of doctrine ever assembled by human acumen and ingenuity. He thought of the mind as a central organ which registers and processes the messages conveyed to it by the five senses, by the feelings of pleasure and pain, and by the innate ideas, which, as if instinctive, exist in advance of experience and so anticipate it. Thus there were three criteria of truth: Sensations, Feelings, and Anticipations.

Such, in brief, was the package of doctrine but among educated people of the time the Sensations had come to stand for the whole package, especially for the reason that this criterion was the most open to attack by the Platonists and Stoics, who exalted reason as a criterion. Among the Sensations, in turn, the sense of sight is so superior to the remaining four that even it was on occasion made to stand for the whole package, as in Colossians 2:18, "taking his stand on what he has seen, puffed up without justification by the mind of the flesh."

That the Sensations as criteria were hovering in the mind of Paul as he was erecting his new canon of truth in First Corinthians 2 is made certain in verse 9: "What eye hath not seen nor ear heard nor ever entered into the mind of man, all that God has prepared for them that love him, God has revealed to us through the Spirit." In this quotation we should observe the mention of eye and ear and recall that sight and hearing are foremost among the criteria of Epicurus; neither should we miss the point that the mind in question is "the mind of the flesh," because it was the teaching of Epicurus that the mind was an organ of the body just as the eyes or the ears.

To have hit upon these verses of Isaiah (64:4 and 65:17) must have afforded to Paul an exquisite satisfaction. It furnishes Old Testament authority for rejecting both the Epicurean criteria and the Epicurean psychology while at the same time naming the new criterion, the spirit, which we may call spiritual insight. The implied inference is made explicit in the verse following: "For the Spirit searches everything, even the depths of God." Here it may be more precise for the sake of the emphasis to read the verse as follows: "For it is the Spirit that searches everything."

It may now seem ironical that Paul, after scorning the criteria of Epicurus, should proceed to reason about his new criterion after the fashion of Epicurus. The latter reasoned as follows: Nothing can refute the sensations; they cannot refute one another. To invent an example, if the nose registers the odor of peppermint, the ears cannot contradict it. Conversely, if the ears register recognition of a melody, the nose cannot contradict them. Neither can the mind contradict the nose or the ears, because by itself it is not cognizant of odors or melodies but depends upon the senses for its information of such. Each of the senses, then, possesses exclusive authority over the phenomena of which it is cognizant and by virtue of this fact gains the status of a criterion. Nothing can refute them.

Now this is precisely the sort of authority that Paul claims for spiritual insight, verse 15: "The spiritual man judges all things but is himself judged by no one." Thus spiritual insight is set up as a criterion of truth, subject to the test of no other criterion. We must consequently correct the translation of the sentence that follows and instead of "For who has known the mind of the Lord so as to instruct him," we had better read, "so as to put it to the proof."

Having by this time clearly apprehended that Paul, like Epicurus before him, is setting up a canon of truth, we become qualified to make another correction. Verse 13 runs as follows in the Revised Standard: "And we impart this in words not taught by human wisdom but taught by the Spirit, *interpreting spiritual truths to those who possess the Spirit.*" Of the phrase in italics two alternative versions are offered in a footnote, all three being erroneous. The Greek word which is here rendered "interpreting" is employed by Epicurus and others in the sense of "matching," and we arrive at the true meaning by reading, "matching the spiritual with the spiritual."

In other words, the criterion that is employed must "match" the truth that is tested; on the level of spiritual truth the criterion of spiritual insight alone is valid. It is tacitly allowed that on other levels of thought other criteria may possess validity, such as the criteria of sight and hearing on the sensory level, but on the spiritual level the sole criterion is spiritual insight, the gift of God.

Even a minor error of translation may be worth correction. The Revised Standard renders verse 14 as follows: "The unspiritual man does not receive the gifts of the Spirit of God, for they are folly to him." The error here is one that frequently occurs, mistaking an idiom of characterization for a statement of fact. Epicurus writes in similar language "that the gods are receptive toward men resembling themselves." So we may improve our translation by reading: "The unspiritual man is unreceptive toward the gifts of the Spirit of God." Paul is informing us how the lack of the proper criterion reacts upon the individual; he becomes prejudiced in advance against spiritual truths because according to his own criteria they are folly.

## Epicurus and Paul and the Soul

The illustrious fifteenth chapter of First Corinthians, where Paul touches his highest point, whether of eloquence or reasoning, is still marred by some imprecisions of interpretation. These may be cured by recognition of the fact that he is arguing against the Epicureans, whose ridicule concentrated itself upon the prophecy of the resurrection, just as their logic of the atom claimed the maximum of certainty for itself in denying immortality. Here, as nowhere else so manifestly, may we discern this logic of the atom in competition with the logic of the cross.

The explanation of these residual obscurities may be found in certain assumptions of Paul, which were justified in his day as matters of common knowledge, though long since lost from view in a despised and neglected tradition of learning. Foremost among these neglected items of tradition is the Epicurean lore of the soul, of which the key word in Paul's language is *psychikos* in Greek, that is, "psychic," but utterly different in force from our modern word of the same spelling.

Epicurus based his whole system of knowledge upon belief in the atom as the ultimate existence and from this he deduced the mortality of the soul as being by nature a subtle atomic compound. This doctrine gained for itself such wide acceptance that the adjective *psychic*, from *psyche*, "soul," became the antonym of *spiritual*, as in the Epistle of Jude, verse 19, where the Revised Standard renders it "worldly": "worldly people, devoid of the Spirit." This rendering possesses merit as a translation and may be adequate for the general reader but greater exactitude is possible. Jude has really furnished us with a precise definition. The "psychic people" are animated only by the mortal soul, *psyche*, and are "devoid of the Spirit" which animates the person who has experienced the rebirth and thereby attains to immortality.

That Jude had the Epicureans in mind is made clear in the preceding verse: "In the last time there will be scoffers, following their own ungodly desires." The mention of ridicule is the identifying badge for the sect.

It was they who had gained for this concept of the soul its currency in the public mind and a brief account of its development will be helpful. Plato, against whom Epicurus was in rebellion, had taught that the soul is immortal and passed from body to body by a series of reincarnations. The retort of Epicurus to this may be read in one of his sayings: "We have been born once and we cannot be born twice, but to all eternity must be no more."

Plato had also looked upon the soul as imprisoned in the body and in consequence invited his disciples to indulge in a certain self-pity. The intrepid Epicurus, on the contrary, looked upon the soul as an equal partner with the body, as being conceived in the womb along with it, born with it, and sharing childhood, adolescence, maturity, and senility with it, and dying with it.

He thought of life as a reciprocation of function between body and soul, each dependent upon the other. His own words may be quoted in part: "The soul must be regarded as the chief cause of sensation; it would not, however, possess this capacity unless it were, so to say, enveloped by the rest of the organism; and the rest of the organism, while bestowing this capacity upon the soul, also acquires for itself from it a share in such contingent capacity."

The effect of this argument is to place body and soul upon a parity. Both are corporeal and depend upon each other for their functioning. Thus the contrast between body and soul is diminished and this fact is reflected in the language of the New Testament. The new contrast is between the flesh and the spirit. The word *flesh* was a key word in the writings of Epicurus long before the times of the New Testament. Space for one example may be spared: "The cry of the flesh is not to hunger, not to thirst, not to suffer from cold." It is true, of course, that flesh and spirit are contrasted in the Old Testament, but to stress the point is to place small change on the collection plate; in the New Testament the contrast has become a necessity of thought, much more than a vivid figure of speech.

114

Another effect, and the more fruitful of consequence, of this parity of soul and body, both being corporeal and mortal, is to evoke the meaning that rightly puzzles the translators in the interpretation of *psychikos*. In First Corinthians 2:14 the King James Version renders it "natural" and the Revised Standard "unspiritual": "The unspiritual (natural) man does not receive the gifts of the Spirit of God." An example upon which the truth hinges still more occurs in the same Epistle, 15:44, where "physical" is read by the Revised Standard: "It is sown a physical body, it is raised a spiritual body."

All three of these renderings, "natural," "unspiritual," and "physical," not to omit the fourth, in Jude 19, "worldly," are for practical purposes commendable but still they are makeshifts. Their deficiency becomes manifest in 15:44, where the Revised Standard reads: "If there is a physical body, there is also a spiritual body." This makes sense but the sense it conveys is not Paul's. What Paul was saying is this: "If there is a body animated by a mortal soul, there is also a body animated by an immortal spirit."

The deficiency becomes even glaring in the next verse, which reads in the Revised Standard: "The first man Adam became a living being; the last Adam became a life-giving spirit." If this makes sense, the sense is not self-evident, certainly not to the general reader. Paul is accepting the doctrine that the *psyche* is corporeal and mortal; in contrast to this stands the eternal spirit, which Christ not only received but along with it the power to bestow it. Hence we may suggest: "The first man Adam was created to be animated by a mortal soul; the last Adam was born to be animated by a life-giving spirit." This may lack the virtue of brevity but the obscure can rarely be stated briefly.

The thesis here being expounded by Paul is baffling, though less because of difficulty than because of its paradoxical character. We have become so thoroughly indoctrinated with belief in the immortality of the soul that to think of Paul entertaining a different view seems preposterous. Yet this is the truth. He concedes to his Greek adversaries the mortality of the soul and then escapes from the consequences of his concession by positing two stages in creation, typified by the first man Adam and the last Adam: "It is not the spiritual that is first but the psychical, and the spiritual afterward." The first stage is that of the *psyche*, the second that of the *pneuma*. The first did not bring immortality; this came by gift of God at the second stage of creation.

Thus Paul deprived the enemies of the cross of Christ of all the logical advantage they had gained in plying the public mind for three hundred years with evidences of the corporeality of the soul. The arguments of Epicurus had become outdated through the miracle of the resurrection of Jesus the Christ. The crucial sentence quoted above may be paraphrased: "I am not claiming that the spirit came first in order of time but I am telling you that the corporeal soul (*psyche*) came first and the spirit at a later date."

Thus the logic of the cross achieves victory over the logic of the atom.

## In the Body or Out of the Body

As yet, however, we have more to learn about the lore of the soul according to Epicurus. There is a second assumption of Paul that calls for accounting. In the same context in which Epicurus essays to demonstrate the parity of partnership between soul and body he insists at some length upon the impossibility of either existing after separation from the other. The soul is described as composed of the finest and most mobile atoms and must be contained and restrained within the body, which functions as a vessel. If the bodily vessel is ruptured, then the soul disperses like water when the pitcher is broken at the fountain.

This particular doctrine was not only notorious; it was also long-lived and suggested to Dante a unique irony of punishment. In the sixth circle of his Inferno the guide exhibited to him a cemetery of lidless coffins, in which the godless Epicureans on the day of the resurrection were to be imprisoned along with their own souls, because they had denied that the soul could exist apart from the body.

Let us now turn to Paul. In Second Corinthians 12:2–3 he writes: "I know a man in Christ who fourteen years ago was caught up to the third heaven — *whether in the body or out of the body I do not know*, God knows — and he heard things that cannot be told."

Why should Paul have interposed that saving clause? He repeats it in the next verse verbatim, which testifies to his concern over the idea. The answer is not difficult. He is protecting himself in advance against the embarrassing questions of the Epicureans, the same who demand to know in First Corinthians 15:35: "How are the dead raised? With what kind of body do they come?" In this instance they would have been bantering him with the question: "When you ascended to the third heaven, were you in the body or out of the body?"

Paul assumes that his readers knew of this doctrine, that the soul cannot exist apart from the body. The modern reader must habituate himself to accept the assumption of its having been as well known in Paul's time as the doctrines of Freud are known today.

## Corruption and Incorruption

This famous fifteenth chapter of First Corinthians is singular for the fact that in verse 52 the word *atom* occurs, the sole example in the Bible. It is hidden for the English reader in the translation, "in a moment," which is amplified in the words "in the twinkling of an eye"; but the Greek reads "in an atom," curiously used by Paul to denote a minimum interval of time, though strictly signifying the minimum particle of matter.

This seems like a trivial clue but it furnishes a precious hint of the identity of the adversaries against whom Paul is arguing, that is, the Epicureans, the champions of the atomic theory of the constitution of matter. This assumption is confirmed by the brandishing of the words *corruption* and *incorruption,* upon which the writings of Epicurus had conferred a universal vogue in the ancient world. Unwittingly Epicurus had prepared the word *incorruption* for its role of denoting a blessed concept in Christian thought. We still pay him a backhanded compliment whenever this consoling chapter is read in our funeral services.

If this thought is somewhat startling, Paul's very first step in the argument by which he essays to demonstrate the doctrine of immortality may be even more so. The questions posed by the unnamed but well-known adversaries are these: "How are the dead raised? With what kind of body do they come?" Paul's very first appeal is to the authority of Nature, which according to Epicurus furnished all the criteria of truth: "You foolish man! What you sow does not come to life unless it dies."

In general it may well astonish and enlighten us to observe how Paul forgets himself and reverts to his Epicurean youth. It seems second nature to him to write in Romans 1:26 and 11:24 "contrary to nature," and in Romans 11:21 and 24 "according to nature." In this very Epistle to the Corinthians, 11:14, he may be found employing the expression,

"Does not Nature herself teach you?" Was it not Epicurus who regarded Nature as the supreme teacher? In the Gospels, on the contrary, not a single occurrence of this word *nature* may be found, not even in that of Luke, Paul's constant companion.

Moreover, when Paul resorts to the comparison between the death of the seed and the death of the body, he is not only appealing to Nature as a norm of truth; he is also drawing a parallel between a natural phenomenon and an event of the spiritual life. This is reasoning by analogy, a method much favored by Epicurus.

It will be both interesting and rewarding to take the next item of argument and observe Paul making himself "as a Greek to the Greeks," verse 39: "For not all flesh is alike, but there is one kind for men, another for animals, another for birds, and another for fish."

This ground had been thoroughly gone over by Epicurus in demonstrating the prevalence of natural law in the physical world as opposed to divine creationism. In his view of things the sole creatrix was Nature. She was the aggregate of all natural laws and allowed no room for miracles. Cats were never born of rabbits nor were rabbits born of cats. Each species of animal was governed by the laws that applied to it. Moreover, each species had its own habitat: fish were not found in treetops nor antlered stags in the depth of the sea.

Paul adopts this line of reasoning with suitable but slight variations and extends it to celestial bodies: "There is one glory of the sun, another glory of the moon," and so on. This extension is poetical and has the desired effect of conferring a certain sublimity upon the passage. It may have captured the imagination of the contemporary reader, and, if so, the success of it would have depended upon the adroit transition from the familiar to the unfamiliar.

The next step in the reasoning, artfully postponed by the little interlude of the sublime and poetical, presents itself in verse 44: "If there is a psychical body, there is also a spiritual body." This too is an adroit extension of the familiar to the unfamiliar, and when we say familiar, we mean familiar to the literate man of Paul's day, because it is no longer familiar to us, however learned. It calls for elucidation.

It was by this identical reasoning that Epicurus strove to demonstrate the existence of the incorruptible. His argument may be expressed in the very same shape of sentence: "If there is a corruptible body, there must also be an incorruptible body." The procedure is known as arguing from the nature of the visible to the nature of the invisible, of which Paul elsewhere reveals his knowledge by employing the same terminology as Epicurus.

In this particular instance the reasoning may be expanded as follows. In certain of the Authorized Doctrines the principle was stated that the universe is infinite in extent. This principle, Epicurus assumed, must apply to values no less than to matter and space. In other words, if imperfection prevailed throughout the whole universe, the universe would not be infinite. Now, in this world which we inhabit he believed it a mere matter of observation "that the forces of destruction always prevail over the forces of creation." Consequently, he deduced the inference that somewhere else there must be a region where "the forces of preservation always prevail over the forces of destruction." This region he identified as "the spaces between the worlds," because he assumed that in an infinite universe there must be numberless worlds more or less like our own.

In the domain of organic life he assumed the existence of an ascending scale of creation, of which, in worlds like our own, mankind was the peak and crown. Human beings, however, by the misfortune of living in a world where the forces of destruction always prevail in the end over the forces of creation, were doomed to mortality. In other words, their bodies were corruptible. Only in the regions between the worlds could incorruptible beings exist and these were, of course, the gods.

Of this reasoning Paul assumes the validity. He merely extends it with the needful modifications of terminology. There are two regions, just as in the universe of Epicurus, earth and heaven. There are two kinds of beings also, the corruptible and the incorruptible, but the incorruptible has a new name: it is the spiritual. Paul even accepts, as shown in the previous section, the doctrine of Epicurus that the soul of man, *psyche*, is corporeal and mortal.

While adducing proof of the existence of the spiritual body, according to a logic familiar to his readers, Paul is at no pains to describe it and this fact may be significant; it seems to have been an assumption too general to require mention that divinity was associated with light. In Philippians 3:20–21 he writes: "who will change our lowly body to be like his glorious body." Our information about the Epicurean heavens and the incorruptible gods is not abundant but we do know that the bodies of these gods were translucent and their abode was one of perpetual light. Paul seems consequently to be assuring his converts that after the miracle of the resurrection it would be their portion to enjoy for ever and ever the same sort of existence which Epicureans believed to be reserved for their blissful and incorruptible gods.

## The Last Enemy

In verse 26 Paul writes: "The last enemy to be destroyed is death." The view of Epicurus was not dissimilar. From the pen of Metrodorus, who was often empowered by the master to speak for the sect, we have these words: "Against all else it is possible to establish security, but as for death, so far as concerns it, all of us human beings inhabit a city without walls." The most arduous of tasks for the resolute and dauntless Epicurus was to liberate man from the fear of death and reconcile him to mortality.

The gist of his conclusion is embodied in the second of his Authorized Doctrines, one of the most publicized sayings in all ancient thought: "Death is nothing to us, because dissolution is the loss of consciousness and unconsciousness is nothing to us." We also possess an exhortation of his which enlarges somewhat upon this sentiment: "Habituate yourself to the thought that death is nothing to us, because all good and evil lie in consciousness and death is the loss of consciousness. Consequently a right understanding of the fact that death means nothing to us renders enjoyable the mortality of life, not by the addition of infinite time but by taking away the yearning for immortality. For there is nothing to fear in living for the man who has thoroughly grasped the idea that there is nothing to fear in not living."

In pursuance of this arduous task of subduing the last enemy the diligent Epicurus also analyzed with his customary acumen the feelings of the worldly man in anticipation of death. These he found to be three: ingratitude, self-pity, and fear. Ingratitude for past blessings inclines the man to shrink from death as the end of all pleasure. Self-pity leads him to dwell in his mind upon mortality, the funeral pyre, and the chill and damp of the tomb. The consciousness of wrongdoing causes him to be haunted by fear of punishment after death.

All of these miseries are ascribable to what Epicurus called "false opinions" and these can be cured by right reason. The whole experience of man, according to Epicurus, can be controlled and must be kept in control. For example, the fear of punishment after death can be dispelled by the knowledge that the gods are incapable of anger and indifferent to the affairs of mankind. Self-pity in the face of death can be cured by the knowledge that death is sheer unconsciousness. The misery of ingratitude can be forestalled by diligent cultivation of the memory of past blessings.

Even after this diligent reasoning there was something lacking, some counterpoise needed for the surrender of immortality. This is furnished in an Authorized Doctrine, which reads: "Infinite time and finite time are characterized by equal pleasure if one measures the limitations of pleasure by reason." This means that the pleasures of life have a limit and, if the individual has so planned his life as to have enjoyed the fullness of pleasure, which is the fullness of happiness, he cannot exceed this limit in eternal life.

## Victory over Death

Epicurus in another Authorized Doctrine insists that it is the flesh that finds the limits of pleasure boundless and yearns for eternal life, which may remind us of Paul's dictum in Galatians 5:17: "For the desires of the flesh are against the Spirit, and the desires of the Spirit are against the flesh." In the reasoning of Epicurus, however, the antithesis is between the flesh and the mind or intellect. The individual who has soberly reasoned the problem out reflects that he has enjoyed the fullness of pleasure in this life and fearlessly faces death. He has achieved what to Paul is victory over death.

The consequence is that the good Epicurean takes leave of life with a cry of triumph. This is the case with the old man of Oenoanda, who caused the doctrines of Epicurus to be inscribed on stone in the market place of his native town, not far from Colossae. We possess a similar record from the pen of Metrodorus, known as a second Epicurus: "When necessity calls upon us to depart, spitting lustily upon life and upon those who madly cling to it, we shall take our leave of living with a glorious paean of victory, hymning the refrain that we have lived the good life."

Since this refrain was widely known, it is no accident that Paul, who has been expounding the new doctrine of immortality with a steadily rising elevation of thought, should crown this exposition with his own paean of victory: "Death is swallowed up in victory," and "O death, where is thy sting? O grave, where is thy victory?" Paul, however, is a careless citator when he quotes the Old Testament and a consultation of the usual references in the concordances to Isaiah and Hosea uncovers no mention of the sting of death.

Luckily we know that this originated with the Epicureans, probably with Epicurus himself. At any rate, we find it in the concluding passage of the third book of Lucretius, where the feelings of the worldly man are analyzed as he contemplates the approach of death. It will be rewarding to scrutinize this analysis anew; our understanding of the sting may be modified and improved.

As it turns out, it is not the sting as of an insect, sudden, sharp, and single, as we may have thought. It is rather the continuous goading that comes of unhappy thoughts, ingratitude, self-pity, and fear of the hereafter. The Greek or Latin word that we translate as "sting" means also the goad with which oxen are driven to the plow; it was of wood, whittled to a point and applied again and again. It was this incessant repetition of the pain and not its intensity that the original metaphor was intended to convey.

Paul amplifies his paean of victory in a single sentence: "The sting of death is sin, and the power of sin is the law." In this the sole word that is alien to Epicureanism is *sin*; in that pagan creed no divine law was recognized and for that reason there was no concept of sin. This fact, however, makes little difference in the psychology of guilt; the Greek no less than the Jew could be goaded by the fear of punishment for the violation of law. Paul is here forgetting himself and speaking as an Old Testament Jew or a pagan. Had he been speaking as a Christian according to his own structure of doctrine, no mention of law would have been needful, because it had been superseded. In his new structure of doctrine the cardinal offense had become the refusal to recognize the resurrected Christ, and it was not sinners but unbelievers who were to be destroyed on the last day.

Since Paul is not speaking consistently with himself, it should not be surprising that the meaning of his words, "the power of sin is the law," may be readily explained by reference to Epicurus, who deals with this idea in two of his Authorized Doctrines. In one of these he writes: "Violating the law is not an evil in itself but the evil lies in the uneasy feeling, of the nature of fear, that he may not escape detection by those appointed for the punishment of such offenses." In the second Doctrine he writes that the wrongdoer "cannot have confidence that he will escape detection, even if ten thousand times he does escape for the time being, because to the day of death it will be uncertain whether to the last he will escape."

Having now learned from Epicurus how the law operates as the power behind sin or wrongdoing, we are qualified to cast a glance of scrutiny at the previous clause, "the sting of death is sin." In this case we may trace both the word and idea to Epicurus. According to his analysis of the feelings of the foolish old man at the approach of death it is the consciousness of wrongdoing and the fear of punishment for the same in the life hereafter that bestows upon death its power to goad its prospective victim. It may even be better for the sake of precision to revise the translation and read: "The goad of death is sin."

If now we attempt the customary backward glance over this chapter we should first recall the principle that a positive declaration presumes its opposite: "the logic of the cross" presumes the existence of the un-named logic of the atom.

Next we should recall that "the logic of the cross" achieves its victory over its competitor by the assumption of two stages of creation, the one characterized by the corporeal and mortal soul, *psyche*, the other characterized by the immortal spirit. The concept of immortality that Epicurus derided has become outdated; a new concept of immortality has been launched, to which the old arguments will not apply.

Of less importance, though helpful in any understanding of Paul's mind and its working, is his conformance with the Epicurean practice of concluding with a paean of victory over death.

Lastly, we have found Paul throughout his argument adopting the procedures of his competitor, even to the extent of appealing to Nature as a source of truth and incorporating Epicurean ideas in his paean of victory. This phenomenon was destined to repeat itself. The African churchmen Arnobius and Lactantius create the impression in the minds of informed readers of knowing their Epicureanism at least as well as their Bibles.

# VIII

# FIRST CORINTHIANS 13

## Faith, Hope, and Love

W<small>HEN</small> the prophet Elisha healed the leprosy of Naaman the Syrian without touch or even presence there was no mention of faith.

When the Roman centurion begged for the healing of his servant in a similar way, Jesus exclaimed: "Truly, I say to you, not even in Israel have I found such faith."

If the word *faith* were proportionately as frequent in the Old Testament as in the New, there would be some seven hundred occurrences. Actually there is one example.

This astonishing emergence of the word *faith* is but one outstanding feature of the revolution of thought that took place in the interval between the Old and the New Testaments.

In this study the assumption is made that this revolution was in the main a consequence of the impact of Greek skepticism upon Jewish culture and in particular of the scientific materialism of Epicurus.

The instinctive reaction of orthodox Judaism to Epicureanism was total rejection; the very name of Epicurus in the form of *apikoro* was adopted into the Hebrew tongue as a synonym for unbeliever. Jewish students were exhorted "to master Torah so as to be able to answer the Epicurean." This reaction is comparable to the revulsion of modern fundamentalism from the theory of biological evolution.

The reaction of Jesus and Paul to Epicureanism was complex and contradictory. By their time, total rejection had become unimaginable, because the busy Greeks had explored the whole domain of ethics with a mathematical thoroughness unknown to the authors of Psalms and Proverbs; and their findings were available in brief and well-written textbooks that were adapted to catch the interest of literate and intelligent people everywhere. The pious Jew would have memorized much sage advice about anger, as in Psalm 37:8: "Cease from anger and forsake wrath"; his Greek friend, however, would give him a booklet of Philodemus to read, with the title *On Anger*, in which the reactions of all classes of men to this disturbing emotion were systematically analyzed. This booklet is still extant in fragments.

Again, in the Old Testament there is an abundance of warnings against the deceitfulness of riches, as in Proverbs 11:28: "He that trusteth in his riches shall fall." The friendly Greek, however, would pass on to his Jewish neighbor for reading a systematic treatise entitled *On Wealth* from the pen of Metrodorus, in which the reactions of poverty and riches upon the happiness of the individual were systematically studied. This book is lost to us, but Epicurus had written on the same subject and an excerpt that survives may be quoted as a specimen: "Poverty, if measured by the end of Nature, is great wealth but unlimited wealth is great poverty."

In truth, if we survey the whole body of Epicurean writings on ethics, we may appraise it as a veritable supplement to the best elements of the Wisdom Literature of the Jews. It campaigned, in particular, against the deceitfulness of wealth, glory, and power, which reflects itself abundantly in the Gospels.

Over against this extensive agreement in practical morality, which was at times extremely embarrassing, stood a total opposition in respect of theology and the motivation of conduct. Epicurus denied all interest or participation on the part of the gods in the affairs of this world. Long before the time of Jesus he had been ridiculing prophecy and miracles. His disciples in Thessalonica ridiculed the prediction by Paul of the second coming of Christ. In Athens they "mocked" at the mention of the resurrection of the dead. This persistent campaign of mockery is reflected by the vehemence with which Jesus asserted the fatherhood of God and by the persistence with which Paul preached the doctrine of grace.

It is in such a clash and tension of creed against creed that new doctrines are born, that virtues previously unhonored are exalted to top importance, and that ideas once commonplace acquire the status of blessed concepts. So long as miracles were accepted as being within the order of things, as in the time of Elisha, there was no need even to make mention of faith. When once, however, the belief in miracles became the target of deliberate mockery, as was the practice of the Epicureans, then faith was speedily exalted to the rank of a virtue.

Yet to this general statement a momentous addition must be made. Miracles of healing were no novelty to the Greeks; to this day they are documented in inscriptions on stone from the shrine of Asclepius, patron god of physicians, at Epidaurus in Greece. The resurrection of the dead, on the contrary, and in particular a universal resurrection of the dead, was a supermiracle, the miracle of miracles. To believe in this required a faith exceeding all previous demands upon faith. Thus mockery became all the more vigorous — such a faith was foolishness to the Greeks — and, as the vigor of mockery increased, all the more emphasis was bound to be placed upon the virtue of faith.

If doubt should exist that the Epicureans were ridiculing the Jews for their belief in miracles, this may perhaps be dispelled by a singular item of evidence from ancient Italy, and that too at a date close to the birth of Christ.

In the year 37 B.C. a meeting was arranged between Mark Antony and the younger Caesar to take place at Tarentum for the purpose of dividing the government between them. Antony's party was coming from the East by sea, Caesar's supporters by land from Rome. While one group of the latter paused at a small town near the modern Bari, the priests of a local shrine undertook to stage a miracle for their diversion; the incense on the altar was to ignite without the application of flame. This was the signal, as the Roman poet Horace relates it, for a round of laughter and witticisms. "Let the Jew Apella believe it," he adds, "not I."

Indeed it might almost appear that the poet had knowledge of the miracle invoked by the prayer of Elias in First Kings 18:38, where it reads: "The fire of the Lord fell and consumed the burnt sacrifice." At any rate, he wrote: "For I have learned the lesson that the gods pass a life untroubled by concern and, if Nature does perform some wonder, it is no frowning gods that send it down from their lofty mansion in the sky."

In expressing this sentiment he was quoting almost verbatim the Epicurean poet Lucretius, who had died only a few years before. It may be added that Horace's own outlook on life was largely Epicurean and at the time of the incident he was in Epicurean company.

From this story the inference may be drawn that if in distant Italy before the birth of Christ the Jews were being ridiculed for their belief in miracles, how much more would this have been true in Palestine, where Epicureanism had been flourishing for at least two centuries, and must have been flourishing all the more as numerous Greek cities were being founded or refounded across the Jordan River in the very century of the nativity.

## Structures of Thought

In order to understand the clash between Epicureanism and Christianity it must be recognized first of all that a philosopher, such as Epicurus, organizes his thought into what may be called a conceptual scheme. At any rate, the logician would so describe it. By the semanticist the same scheme would be styled a structure of meanings or a matrix of meanings. Whatever it be called, however, the concepts that are built into the scheme are arranged around some central concept as the parts of the atom are arranged around the nucleus. Each concept takes its meaning from its part in the scheme.

This abstract statement may be transferred from the realm of philosophy or semantics to that of common knowledge by recounting what Epicurus had to say about faith, which was considerable. In his thinking, the central or nuclear concept was called "ataraxy," which means the peace of mind that comes of freedom from all disturbing thoughts. In order to enjoy this peace the individual must be free from fear of fate, from fear of Fortune, from fear of divine wrath, and from fear of death and the hereafter. In order to be free from these fears, in turn, man must have faith in the truth of doctrine. To furnish the foundations of faith Epicurus composed numerous handbooks and in particular he drew up his list of forty Authorized Doctrines, which were an anticipation of Articles of Faith in the later Christian church.

A few particulars will further clarify the meaning of the above. According to Greek myths it was the destiny of Achilles to die by a wound in his heel and of Oedipus to slay his own father and marry his own mother. These are examples of fate. All such stories were dismissed as silliness by Epicurus. He adduced reasoned proofs that the gods lived aloof from the world and the affairs of mankind.

The physical world, he undertook to prove, was governed by natural

127

laws but even in this doctrine there was something to fear. Certain Greek philosophers had already anticipated certain modern scientists by putting forward a mechanistic theory of the universe, according to which the behavior of the individual was absolutely predetermined by physical laws. Epicurus revolted from this more violently than from divine decrees. To escape from this crippling mechanistic necessity he postulated a sufficient degree of play in the motions of the atoms to permit of free will in man. Thus, according to his thinking, in spite of the fact that the physical universe was governed solely by natural laws, man himself could claim exemption from these laws.

As for Fortune, whom Greeks and Romans revered as a goddess, the bringer of wealth and poverty, freedom and slavery, all fear of her pranks could be forestalled by foresight and preparedness.

Fear of death was nullified by knowledge of the nature of man. The soul was a volatile compound of atoms and subject to dissolution; dissolution, in turn, resulted in unconsciousness and unconsciousness was not to be feared. By the same knowledge fear of the hereafter was canceled. Faith in this knowledge would assure peace of mind.

On the social level the enjoyment of peace of mind was dependent upon the feeling of safety or security, which is a sort of faith. According to Epicurus, this could be assured by systematically cultivating friendships, upon which the individual could count for aid in all the emergencies against which the modern man seeks protection by various forms of paid insurance, by sick benefits, unemployment relief, and pensions. The fact that confident dependence upon this source of aid was recognized by Epicurus as being a form of faith is made manifest by one of his sayings, which is made the more memorable by the play upon words: "We do not so much need help in time of need as faith in help in time of need."

According to his reasoning the chief enemy of peace of mind is uncertainty, the opposite of faith. He thought it worse, for example, to be uncertain whether to believe in judgment after death than either to believe in it or disbelieve it. Again, he thought the reason that crime does not pay is the very uncertainty of punishment. If this seems a negative sort of teaching the positive aspect of it is also clearly expressed in Authorized Doctrine 17: "The just life knows the most perfect peace but the unjust life is burdened to the limit with worry." This line of reasoning may suggest to us the words of Paul in Romans 1:17, "The just shall live by faith," and also throw some light upon it.

If a synoptic glance be now cast over all these items of truth concerning faith, it may be seen how they go together to constitute a conceptual scheme, a structure of thought, or a matrix of meanings. The nuclear concept according to Epicurus is ataraxy or peace of mind. Around this may be ranged a galaxy of positive and negative concepts. The negatives are fears: fear of poverty and calamity, fear of fate, fear of vengeful gods, fear of death, and fear of judgment and punishment hereafter. The positive concepts are aspects of faith: faith in friends, faith in the just life, faith in doctrine concerning the gods, death, and judgment.

Out of this structure of thought there emerges, it must be discerned, a genuine value in matters of conduct, the virtue of faith. Faith is already well on its way to becoming a blessed concept and the word *faith* is well on its way to becoming one of those electrified symbols of thought which are capable of relaying a surge of spiritual feeling never contemplated by Epicurus himself, in spite of the fact that he took the first steps in preparing it to perform this function.

The ethical validity of the truth so erected was too genuine to be rejected by Christianity but the implied theology was too repellent to be tolerated. This repulsion had the effect of throwing Christianity to the opposite extreme, so that, while appropriating the concept of faith, it joined it with miracles, which Epicurus had ridiculed; it joined it with the fatherhood of God and divine providence, concepts which to Epicurus were incompatible with deity. The very vehemence with which Jesus preached these reconstituted concepts is silent testimony to the vigor of the impact exercised upon Judaism in the interval between the Old Testament and the New. In the Old Testament they were mere assumptions; it was the persistent and organized campaign of assault upon them that created a compelling necessity of building them up into an explicit and positive structure of thought.

Naturally this process of erecting the new structure of thought was only the concluding phase of a slow and gradual movement extending over a long period of time. If such movements be graphically charted they take the form of a slowly ascending line, which toward the end begins to rise at a sharper angle until a maximum height is reached. The speed of the change follows a similar law; extremely slow in its first stages, it also accelerates slowly but toward the end begins to accelerate more rapidly until at last the phenomenon ends explosively.

If now an attempt be made to fit the history of the idea of faith into this pattern, the outcome will be as follows. Of that extended period of time during which the movement was very slowly gathering altitude and speed, we have an imperfect record; it transpired in the two centuries between the Old and New Testaments. All that we possess in the record is the social and religious revolution with which it terminated. This is recorded for us in the stories of Jesus and Paul. At the beginning faith was an assumption; at the end faith had become a doctrine. The idea of faith has been elevated to the rank of a blessed concept and the term *faith* had been enrolled in the chorus of blessed words.

Even in our scant records there are two phases in the history of the idea and both of them are somewhat explosive, even if today this hardly seems to be true. Jesus took pains to give the impression that he had come not to destroy, but to fulfill. It was not an innovation when he demanded belief in the fatherhood of God and his providence; this was implied in the old religion; all that was new was the demand for a fresh emphasis and a fresh vitality of belief. When, on the other hand, he demanded faith in himself, which he did constantly, this was revolutionary and the end result of this demand was the crucifixion.

The second and final phase of the history of the idea — and the more revolutionary — was an inevitable sequel of the previous phase. What Paul demanded was faith in the resurrection of Christ as an event historically authenticated. The reality of this event was construed by him as the guarantee of the second coming, the general resurrection, and the exaltation of believers. It should hardly be needful to quote First Corinthians 15:14: "And if Christ be not risen, then is our preaching vain, and your faith also is vain."

The assent to belief in the resurrection of Christ as an historical event is the act of faith with which the religious experience begins; this experience proceeds, as described in Romans 1:17, "from faith to faith"; it finds its fruition in the state of perfect faith that is "the peace of God." Thus, as we may read in Hebrews 12:2, Jesus is "the author and finisher of our faith," though it would be more precise to read, "the beginner and the finisher."

On this topic there is still a note to be added. Although Epicurus has been denied much influence upon the growth of religion, the atomic theory of matter, which he espoused, was making a smart impact on the study of medicine. It was an atomist, for instance, if not certainly an Epicurean, Erasistratus by name, who first traced the trunk nerves to the brain. It also fell to his lot to give an impulse to the movement that exalted the spirit of man as opposed to the soul, which we can discern in operation in Paul's thinking. The tendency had long flourished of associating the breath of life with the air of the atmosphere but men knew they must be different. This Erasistratus thought to solve the puzzle by proposing that the air was transformed in the heart into the vital breath. This was merely one facet of a drift of thought that presented many aspects. It contributed to the vogue of the word *spirit*, Latin *spiritus*, "breath," without which little thinking could be done in the realm of religion.

## Hope

The emergence of hope as a virtue exhibits a pattern similar to that of faith but with a surprising difference. In this instance the significant contrast is not between the Old and the New Testament but rather between the Gospels on the one hand and Acts and the Epistles on the other. The noun *hope* is not found in the Gospels. Jesus had little to say about the life hereafter and nothing about the hope of it. The determining factor in his thinking is an event in the present: "The kingdom of heaven is at hand." His teachings constitute a gospel of the present and not of the future; his mind is preoccupied by the urgency of the present and not of the future; the immediate demand is for repentance and belief, which raises procrastination to the rank of a cardinal sin. Hope is virtually forgotten.

In the processes of Paul's thought, on the contrary, the determining factors are two: first, the belief in an event in the past, the resurrection of Christ; and second, the expectation of an event in the future, the second coming and the general resurrection. These two events are complementary to each other and the faith in the one is correlative to the hope of the other. Thus faith and hope become an inseparable pair.

Next, as will be shown with more explicitness in the following chapter, faith and hope are virtues of the interim of time between the two resurrections and their validity will terminate with the event that terminates the interim, the second coming, which will justify the faith and fulfill the hope. For this reason in First Corinthians 13:13 these two are made to rank lower than love, which is of the nature of God himself and eternal. This beloved verse, however, must be translated anew in order to make this interpretation clear. This correction will be made in due course.

It follows from all this that the gospel of Paul is essentially one of hope, while that of Jesus is one of repentance. The words *repent* and *repentance* abound in the first three Gospels, while confined in Paul's writings to some seven examples. Contrarily, the verb *hope* is lacking in Matthew and Mark and confined to three examples in Luke and one in John, though abounding in the Pauline writings.

For Paul, therefore, there are two classes of men: those who have hope and "the others who have no hope," as we read in First Thessalonians 4:13. In the class of men without hope the Epicureans were the more conspicuous because they ridiculed all prophecy and in particular the prophecy of the second coming and the general resurrection, which provokes Paul in this same Epistle, 5:3, to express his scorn for them, identifying them by their watchwords Peace and Safety.

This identification should meet with the readier acceptance for the reason that the Stoics had already denounced their more popular rivals as men without hope on the ground of their repudiating divine providence. We learn this from the Stoic philosopher Seneca, who makes it plain that men who reject belief in divine providence can have no hope of benefiting by the goodness of the divine being. Thus it becomes manifest that this characterization of the Epicureans was already part of the public mind of the time and Paul was merely confirming it on novel and more specific grounds.

## The Epicurean Hope

Epicurus, however, had captured the attention of the public mind long before the days of Jesus and Paul and in some essential respects had prefigured the teachings of both. He had the precedence over Jesus, for example, in stamping with emphasis the urgency of the present and in making a cardinal sin of procrastination, but this topic cannot be amplified here. What immediately demands our attention is his precedence over Paul in winning a status of blessedness for the concept of hope. Over the space of three centuries his teachings had been making the ancient public familiar with a philosophy of hope and either fortuitously or providentially preparing the way for the acceptance of a religion of hope.

As was characteristic of all the reasonings of Epicurus, this particular teaching was offered in a neat and attractive package. It presumed for mankind the possession of free will and taught the possibility and necessity of keeping the whole experience of the individual under control. To this end the individual must deliberately choose his attitude toward the past, the present, and the future. The proper attitude toward the past was judged to be gratitude; toward the present, the will to enjoy it to the full; and toward the future, hope.

It is possible to be more specific: by gratitude toward the past is meant the grateful recollection of past pleasures; by hope of the future is meant the happy expectation of pleasures to come.

Thus the virtues of gratitude and hope are complementary to each other and this may well remind us that in Paul's scheme of thought faith and hope are complementary concepts, because faith signifies belief in an event of the past, the resurrection of Christ, and hope signifies belief in an event of the future, the second coming.

The substitution of faith, however, as a concept reciprocal to hope, has a curious consequence. The virtue of gratitude is deprived of a context and is left in isolation. Its validity as a factor of conduct, however, cannot be denied — and in numerous passages Paul urges the giving of thanks — but the giving of thanks becomes a duty of the individual toward God, as in Second Corinthians 9:15: "Thanks be to God for his unspeakable gift!" With Epicurus the attitude of thankfulness is to be cultivated because ingratitude spells misery, especially in old age.

A similar observation may be made concerning hope as a factor of conduct. With Epicurus the virtue of hope is esteemed as a factor of happiness. Pessimistic people are not only unhappy themselves; they also contribute to the unhappiness of others. It is for this reason that an attitude of hopefulness should be adopted and cultivated. Of this Paul shows himself aware in his ecstatic hymn of love, First Corinthians 13; in verse 7 we read: "Love hopeth all things." As will be shown in the next chapter, this verse deals with human relations and this particular clause means that the individual who feels true brotherly love is hopeful under all circumstances and never pessimistic. Thus hope means two things to Paul: first, it is a virtue of conduct day by day; and second, it is the hope of the second coming and its glorious sequels.

## Hope and Health

This account of the virtue of hope would be left one-sided and deficient were we to omit mention of the association of hope with health in the creed of Epicurus. The bearing of this association upon Paul's atti-

133

tudes and reasonings may not be obvious at the outset but this bearing can be demonstrated and the reward will be an improved understanding of the content and workings of Paul's mind.

It will be well to begin with certain words of Epicurus himself. One of his most quoted sayings runs as follows: "The stable condition of sound health in the flesh and the confident hope of this means the height of pleasure and the best assurance of it for those who are able to figure the problem out."

By this time it should not be necessary for us to amplify at length the figuring of the problem. A brief chain argument will suffice: if belief in an afterlife is denied, this mortal life becomes the most precious possession of man; by the same token health becomes equally precious, and the hope of its continuance becomes the greatest of pleasures.

Enemies of Epicurus, and especially the Platonists, retorted that the hope of continuous health was one of the most illusory things in life and they quoted the great physician Hippocrates in support of their thesis. The disciples of Epicurus, nevertheless, continued to follow the master and placed their reliance upon the simple life as the assurance of health.

Welcome corroboration of this teaching was afforded by new tendencies in the practice of medicine, because the atomic theory as espoused by Epicurus had begun from an early date to exert a definite influence upon the art of healing. For example, the renowned medical researcher Erasistratus, who was an atomist, if not certainly an Epicurean, began to lay unprecedented stress upon what we now call therapeutics in the treatment of disease and specifically upon diet and exercise.

These tendencies were manifested also in the activities of Asclepiades, undoubtedly an Epicurean, who lived in Rome, knew the great men of the day, such as Cicero, and became the outstanding physician of the ancient world in the last century B.C. His fame was the greater because he possessed the art of dramatizing himself and on one occasion stopped a funeral procession and revived the corpse. His achievements were nevertheless substantial: he was the first to distinguish clearly between acute and chronic phases of disease and his influence was long-lasting and beneficent in the domain of medical services in the Roman army.

The particular aspect of his innovations that here concerns us was his rebellion against the callousness of physicians and his sympathetic consideration for the feelings and comfort of the patient.

A brief anecdote will at one and the same time serve to exemplify the callousness that was in vogue and remind us usefully of the close association between philosophers and physicians. On a certain occasion the philosopher Antisthenes, from whom the more robust breed of Stoics was said to trace its lineage, was asked why he "lashed out so savagely at his pupils." "Because," he replied, "physicians do the same with the sick." This Antisthenes, by the way, maintained that pain was a good thing and was continually saying, "I would rather go mad than feel pleasure."

Thus both philosophers and physicians were divided two ways according to their attitudes toward pleasure and pain.

One of the innovations of the sympathetic Epicurean physicians was to allow patients the use of wine, and the very fact of this having found a place in the records should remind us how shocking it must have been to old practitioners. Having knowledge of the innovation, however, we may read with more interest and understanding the advice of Paul in First Timothy 5:23: "Do not confine yourself to water any longer but use a little wine because of your throat and your frequent attacks of illness." The word that we inherit as *stomach* means "throat" in good Greek and it seems that Timothy may have suffered from a recurrent trouble in his throat. It is very doubtful that Paul was advising him to use a little wine "for his stomach's sake." He was rather telling him that his malady required no departure from his regular diet.

Paul, like Epicurus himself and the Epicurean physicians, was interested in the subject of diet and his views were liberal, as we may learn from Philippians 4:12, where our accepted versions tend to be evasive. We should rather read: "I know how to eat my fill and how to go hungry." On the teachings of the rival schools about such questions Paul may have learned much from Luke. The very description of this man as "the beloved physician" ought to be sufficient evidence that he was no sponsor of pain as something good. He was notably a sympathetic man, especially toward women, as may be observed in his Gospel, and this particular trait was traditional with Epicureans, who from the first admitted women to the study of their philosophy, while other schools tolerated only the few viragos who possessed the hardihood to force their way in.

If now we make the customary pause for taking our bearings afresh, it will be enlightening to observe the similarity between the Epicurean attitude toward health and the hope of its continuance with a thriving and growing attitude in modern society. Never before in all history have

such concerted efforts been made toward improving and preserving public health and increasing the comfort and security of old age and the
hope of it. It is true that we are not yet stamping the word *Security* upon
our coins, as the Romans in Paul's day were stamping their SECURITAS,
but the word security is already far on its way toward becoming a
blessed concept, just as peace and safety were blessed concepts to the
Epicureans.

In respect of this ancient movement in philosophy and medicine Paul
was, as usual, pulled two ways, one way by the ethic of the thing and the
other way by the logic and motivation of it. He was able to feel in total
sympathy with the increased consideration for the health and comfort
of mankind but was utterly unable to concede to the hope of health and
a happy old age the first place in the expectation of mankind.

To Epicurus, who rejected immortality, the supreme joy might be
the possession of health and the confident hope of its continuance; but
for Paul, who looked forward to eternal life, the keenest emotion was
"the joy of the faith," as in Philippians 1:25 or "joy in the Holy Spirit,"
as in Romans 14:17.

In the respective contexts Epicurus and Paul employ the same Greek
word *chara*. To the one it signified the joy that comes of fullness of life
in the flesh and the hope of it; to the other it signified the joy that comes
of fullness of life in the Spirit and the hope of it. A philosophy of hope
was stimulating the growth of a religion of hope.

## The Love of God

Epicurus thought of himself as a pathfinder in the exploration of truth,
blazing a way for others who might choose to follow in his footsteps.
It was not permissible for Paul as a humble servant of God to lay claim
to such a distinction for himself, but the very diligence with which he
cultivated humility is evidence of his consciousness of faring through
strange seas of thought alone.

There is this further similarity between the two men, at least for those
who appreciate a little subtlety of thought. Epicurus in his eager desire
to dethrone the Platonic reason and exalt Nature and science as the
source of truth, involuntarily placed himself in the paradoxical position
of employing reason to dethrone reason. In like manner Paul, because
of his eager determination to supersede the philosophy of love by the
religion of love, was placing himself in the paradoxical position of rea-

soning after the fashion of the philosopher to overthrow the philosophy itself.

The chief obstacle to our discerning aright the drift of Paul's reasoning arises from our very familiarity with his writings. A particular difficulty arises from the necessity of discerning the unfamiliar negatives that underlie his too familiar positives.

We shall make no mistake, however, if we select as a point of departure his belief in the resurrection of Christ as historical fact. From this beginning a whole chain of argument will lead us aright. This resurrection would not have occurred but for the ministry and crucifixion of Jesus as historically recorded. These, again, would not have come to pass without the love of Christ for mankind. This love, in its turn, would never have existed but for the love of God for mankind, of which it was the manifestation.

By this chain of reasoning we thus arrive at ultimate facts, God and the love of God, beyond which there is no other reality. This conclusion once being reached, we may discern the unfamiliar negative that was at the back of Paul's mind when he pronounced the familiar positive in First Corinthians 1:28, "God chose . . . even things that are not to bring to nothing things that are." This is irony, truth in reverse: the ultimate reality for Epicurus was the atoms, physical realities, ironically "the things that are"; the ultimate realities for Paul were God and the love of God, spiritual realities, ironically "the things that are not." Here we observe the logic of the atom in opposition to the logic of the cross. The latter is the familiar positive, the former the now unfamiliar negative, lost to our knowledge by fault of inherited prejudice.

While the theme of divine love is claiming our attention it may improve our understanding of it to mention an item of Epicurean reasoning that applies here and must have been known to Paul. The proud Plato, who was suspicious of pleasure, held to the view that a virtuous action might or might not be accompanied by pleasure. Epicurus retorted vigorously that virtue and pleasure were inseparable; the good life and the happy life could no more be separated from each other than heat could be separated from fire, whiteness from snow, or sweetness from honey.

No doubt can exist that Paul thought of divine love after the same formula; love is an attribute inseparable from God. One can think of love apart from God but to think of God apart from love is impossible.

It deserves our notice that Paul never goes so far as to identify God with love, as we find this done in First John 4:8: "for God is love." He consistently holds to the view that love is an inseparable attribute of God. He did, of course, identify the love of God with the love of Christ and we shall make an addition to our understanding of divine love if we scrutinize anew the familiar words of Ephesians 3:19: "and come to know the love of Christ, which passes knowledge." This is paradoxical: how can one come to know something that passes knowledge? What is the lurking assumption in this syncopated reasoning?

What Paul silently assumes is the principle that on the spiritual level of knowledge there is only one canon of truth( the gift of the Spirit,) as we find it stated in First Corinthians 2:15: "The spiritual man judges all things, but is himself judged by no one." On another level of knowledge another canon may hold valid; for example, on the level of the concrete the Sensations as espoused by Epicurus may be valid criteria; the criterion of color is in the eyes and the eyes alone. By a like reasoning the knowledge of the love of God is attainable only by the gift of the Spirit and so may be said to pass understanding by any other criterion of truth. Hence the paradoxical idea, "come to know the love of Christ, which passes knowledge." It is understandable through "the wisdom of God" but not through "the wisdom of the world."

This line of reasoning would never have been employed unless Epicurus had first habituated the public mind to the notion of a canon or criterion of knowledge.

We may perhaps arrive at even greater precision in our understanding of divine love if we scan its relationship to faith; and this will bring to our notice yet another of our beloved mistranslations, Galatians 5:6: "For in Christ Jesus neither circumcision nor uncircumcision is of any avail, but faith that worketh through love." Faith by its very nature is an inert thing; it is a passive attitude. If the depositor has faith in his bank, he has no need to take action. It follows that faith, being by nature a passive attitude, stands in need of an activator, and in the sphere of conduct this function is performed by love. Love is a dynamic thing; unless it manifests itself in action, it forfeits its right to the name of love. So the love of Christ may be defined as faith at work.

We may consequently improve our translation by reading: "faith that is activated through love" or "faith that is stimulated to action through love."

We may advance our understanding to yet another notch of exactitude by glancing at the Old Testament. There we shall find that love is demanded by God and required by law, Deuteronomy 6:5: "And thou shalt love the Lord thy God with all thy heart, and with all thy soul, and with all thy might." According to Paul, on the contrary, love is offered rather than demanded by God; all that is required of the individual is to make a voluntary bid for the recognition of God and by virtue of this recognition he begins to participate in the love of God. This idea awaits amplification in the chapter to follow.

We shall also attain a higher degree of clarity if we observe that in the Old Testament we are dealing with a jealous God and a vengeful God, "visiting the iniquity of the fathers upon the children," as we read in Exodus 20:5. This God is also an officer of law enforcement, who holds over violators the threat of punishment: "the Lord will not hold him guiltless that taketh his name in vain," as we read in verse 7 of the above chapter.

This idea of jealous and vengeful gods was merely one item in a comprehensive controversy over the nature of divine beings that flourished throughout the three centuries preceding the times of Jesus and Paul. No better evidence of the existence of this controversy need be cited than the fact that Cicero published a major work entitled *On the Nature of the Gods*. Cicero's voice was never one to be heard crying in the wilderness; no topic was attractive to him until other men had created a market for his views. To illustrate: Epicurus had derided all prophecy; Cicero treated the topic under the heading of Divination.

If reference to conditions in Rome may seem at first sight somewhat farfetched and surprising, we need to be reminded that Rome, even before the Christian era, was part of the market for Greek books and learning. What may well be more surprising, it had become a center of production for Greek books. For example, the writings of the Epicurean physician Asclepiades, who was admired by Cicero himself, were vigorously attacked by the last great medical writer of antiquity, Galen, whose home was in Asia. There is also reason for suspecting that the views of this Asclepiades on diet and the use of wine for the sick were known to Luke and Paul.

Distinctly more significant for the purposes of the present inquiry were the writings of the Epicurean Philodemus, who also enjoyed the respect of Cicero. Though he was writing in Rome, the market for his publications extended eastward over the whole domain of Greek culture. Some of his writings were certainly known to Paul and this may well be true of three volumes composed by him under the title *On the Gods*, still extant in ampler fragments than is usual.

In this work he stressed the friendliness of the gods: "The gods are friends of the wise and the wise are friends of the gods." Moreover, since in the language of Epicurus friendship and love are denoted by one and the same word, we may quite justly amend the above saying to read: "The gods are lovers of the wise and the wise are lovers of the gods."

It follows from this fact that the disciples of Epicurus, long before the days of the New Testament, were habituating the public mind of the time to a concept of divine love that was by no means negligible. Epicurus himself had drilled these disciples to associate no idea with the divine nature that would detract from its sanctity and majesty. In the very first of his Authorized Doctrines he had asserted the immunity of the divine nature to the passion of anger. Anger in the view of the Greeks was a feeling that one had been injured or the fear that one might be injured. How could such a feeling be ascribed to a "blessed and incorruptible being" without detracting from its claim to reverence by man? Anger by its very nature is a confession to weakness, which cannot be associated with a god.

In the light of this information it should not be astonishing that the jealous, wrathful, and threatening Jehovah of the Old Testament has been transformed into the God of love in the New Testament. The concept of the supreme being had changed in pace with the change in the concept of deity in the public mind. All the armament of ridicule and reason that Epicurus had invented to revolutionize the pagan concept of deity was infinitely more applicable to Judaism in later days, because no god in the Greek pantheon had even approximated to the pre-eminence of Jehovah as a lawgiver and a stern officer of law enforcement.

This revolution in the concept of God was bound to raise the logical difficulty of reconciling the previous fear of God with the new love of God. This difficulty is not specifically solved by Paul but did not escape the attention of John, who sometimes cures the omissions of Paul. The solution is found in the first Epistle, fourth chapter, and especially verse 18: "There is no fear in love, but perfect love casteth out fear. For fear has to do with punishment, and he who fears is not perfected in love." Thus Christianity comes around to the position of Epicureanism; Philodemus specifically states that the divine being is not to be feared, though he can love and be loved.

Yet even if Paul omitted to deal specifically with the logical clash between fear and love, it is manifest that the reconciliation of the two with each other had been effected in his own mind. The fear of God in his revised theology is no longer the fear of punishment but merely reverential fear, the fear of God's displeasure. The law has been superseded. God no longer demands and commands the love of man for himself; he makes the offer of his own love to mankind.

## Brotherly Love

It is not astonishing, however, that Paul was not always consistent. He had four personalities to keep in coordination, which originated as follows: from a Jewish childhood; from a Greek adolescence; from graduate study in Jerusalem under Gamaliel, in what an eminent Jewish scholar calls "Talmudic casuistry"; and finally, from his own experience on the road to Damascus.

As a Jewish boy he would have learned the Old Testament stories and memorized the Commandments and much of the law. From this experience would have come the recollection that brotherly love had been commanded in a context of threat and revenge, Leviticus 19:18: "Thou shalt not avenge, nor bear any grudge against the children of thy people, but thou shalt love thy neighbor as thyself: I am the Lord."

This ingrained association of brotherly love with the opposite, the spirit of revenge, asserts itself in the twelfth chapter of Romans. In verse 10 Paul writes: "Love one another with brotherly affection"; and shortly afterward he adds in verse 19: "Beloved, never avenge yourselves, but leave it to the wrath of God; for it is written, 'Vengeance is mine, I will repay, says the Lord'."

If now we turn from this Old Testament habit of opposing brotherly love to vengefulness and cast a scrutinizing glance at Paul's ecstatic hymn to love in First Corinthians 13, we shall discover an opposition of ideas that is quite different. Unselfish brotherly love is set over against the "sounding brass" of self-advertising egotism or arrogance. This is undeniably the Epicurean device of opposing "the vice to the corresponding virtue." Moreover, as will be demonstrated in the following chapter of this study, the beloved verse that begins "Love beareth all things," if rightly interpreted, enshrines four qualities of true love or friendship according to Epicurus.

This may be surprising but yet another surprise is at hand. In the very next verse we read: "Love never ends." This means that love is an attribute of God himself and so is eternal. The man who here speaks is the regenerate Paul, the man who was reborn on the way to Damascus. No other man would have discerned that love is greater than faith and hope, because love is of the nature of God, while faith and hope belong only to the experience of man. This teaching calls for amplification, which may be found in the chapter following.

In the meanwhile it will repay the effort to attempt a retrospective survey of the findings of the present chapter. These findings will perhaps set themselves in order if we examine first the mind of Paul and then the minds of those to whom he addressed his gospel.

We have found Paul to be capable of thinking and writing in four ways: first, as a Jew with orthodox training in childhood; second, as a man of Greek education with liberal tendencies; third, as a pupil of Gamaliel; and lastly, as an individual, a man transformed by a singular and explosive religious experience.

The public mind, by way of contrast, had long been habituated to the point of saturation with the analysis, criticism, and discussion of the essentials of ethics, religion, and irreligion. In this welter of intellectual activity the Epicureans and Stoics alone had positive and practical teachings to offer; but the Stoics, by their asperity and censoriousness and their logic-chopping, limited their appeal and their numbers. The Epicureans, on the contrary, by virtue of their inveterate friendliness and perspicuous reasonings, enjoyed the most numerous following.

It was consequently with this sect that Paul experienced the chief affinity at the same time that it furnished the sharpest criticism and competition. These Epicureans stressed the importance of brotherly love, though they called it friendship. They stressed also the importance of faith, though it meant for them faith in doctrine, faith in leaders, and faith in friends. They stressed also the importance of attitudes: gratitude for past pleasures and the hope of pleasures to come.

This structure of ethics either fortuitously or providentially operated as a bridge of transition to Paul's structure of doctrine. Brotherly love still occupies a foremost position but is transcended by the love of God. Faith in doctrine and in friends is still valid as a factor of conduct but is transcended by faith in the resurrected Christ along with intimations of an expanding religious experience, "from faith to faith." Neither is hope denied its validity in the domain of happy human relations but it acquires a new and specific meaning as the confident expectation of the second coming and its precious implications.

# IX

# FIRST CORINTHIANS 13

## Interim and Recognition

IT IS an astonishing fact — and the earnest student of the New Testament will profit by learning to live with it — that the passages of Paul's Epistles which we most prefer as devotional readings exhibit the most influence of Epicurus.

Among the foremost of these is the hymn to love, the thirteenth chapter of First Corinthians. It falls into two parts: the first seven verses are a unit, as also the last six. The theme of the first unit is brotherly love, which, like faith and hope, should prevail on earth; the theme of the second unit is divine love, which is eternal and will prevail in heaven.

In the hymn as a whole there is a crescendo of interest, importance, and, it must be added, of difficulty. This difficulty has its basis in two hidden assumptions of Paul's thought, without which exact understanding is impossible. The first assumption is that of the interim, which conditions Paul's thinking, the feeling that men of his generation were living under temporary conditions; the second assumption is that of recognition, the belief that mutual recognition occurs between man and God at the moment of profession of faith and continues as a progressive experience in the Christian life, arriving at a climax on the last day, the end of the interim.

The concept of the interim will turn out to be Jewish in origin while the concept of recognition will be identified as a constituent of the philosophy and literature of Greece. The interaction of the two, when once apprehended, will furnish a key to the formulation of Paul's doctrine and exemplify at the same time the process of transition from philosophy to religion.

In the study of brotherly love the chief assistance will come from a knowledge of Epicurean ethics. By the help of this, in particular, the euphonious obscurity of "Love beareth all things" and the rest of verse 7 may be replaced by precision and lucidity.

In the second half of the chapter the chief assistance will come from a knowledge of the teachings of Epicurus about the attitude of the gods toward mankind. To be specific, his assertion of the complete aloofness of the gods to human affairs was a challenge to Paul to assert the recognition of man by God, a doctrine which he elaborated. In this instance the repulsive force of the teaching of Epicurus furnished the stimulus to invent and refine the substitute doctrine.

Lastly, another of our familiar mistranslations, "And now abideth faith, hope, charity," will be corrected in the light of the concept of the interim.

## Sounding Brass

As a prelude to the study of brotherly love an elucidation is due to be made, long overdue, in fact, of the innuendo of "sounding brass" and "tinkling cymbal," with which Paul's hymn begins. In order to rescue this innuendo from the obscurity shed over it by the lapse of time, recourse must be taken to a quick glance at Greek religion.

In the great age of Greece there were but a few oracles, Apollo's at Delphi enjoying a solitary precedence. This was consulted almost exclusively by governments, kings, and princes. In the course of time, as aristocratic societies were leveled down and the political centers of gravity shifted elsewhere, a multitude of local oracles and other devices of prediction rose to popularity. Most of these made a prey of superstitious people, just as organized gambling in our own time makes capital of events in the future for the exploitation of light-minded and improvident individuals.

Some of the new prophetic cults were imported from Asia and Egypt and from the former came the most notorious, the worship of Cybele, so-called Mother of the Gods, chiefly associated with Mount Berecynthus in Phrygia. It was the most notorious because it took the form of a traveling religious circus, going from city to city and bringing prophecy to the door of the consumer, as it were.

The image of the goddess, represented as a portly dame with a turreted crown upon her head, was borne in procession through the streets, bobbing this way and that upon the back of an unfortunate ass. She was accompanied by a throng of weird attendants jangling tambourines, beating drums, clashing cymbals, and blowing huge horns of brass. Flowers and coins were strewn in their path by superstitious multitudes, roused to hysteria by the spectacle of an exotic mystery religion gauged to their own vulgar level. Of this excitement the priests took advantage by telling fortunes for such fees as could be extorted from their victims.

These barbarian priests were infamous for their egotism and effrontery, and all the instruments of their worship became symbols of self-advertising, often known to the ancients as vainglory or self-love. For example, in the very lifetime of Christ there flourished in Rome a Greek poet named Apion, especially notorious for egotism. He was styled by the philosopher Seneca "the drum of his own fame," but it remained for the Emperor Tiberius to dub him, with a grimness of satire characteristic of the Romans, "the cymbal of the universe," which meant the greatest egotist on earth.

This noisy worship of Cybele was in the mind of Paul when he took up his pen to write First Corinthians 13; he was calling attention to a vice in order to gain attention for the corresponding virtue, branding with scorn the self-advertising egotism of the pagan priests in order to gain increased esteem for self-obliterating brotherly love. It is consequently an error to follow the Revised Standard Version and change "sounding brass" to a "noisy gong." The reference is to the huge brass horn — really of bronze — of Cybele's worshipers, which was an object of common knowledge. Even in Rome it had the same significance, as is evidenced by lines of the poet Horace, who died a scant four years before the birth of Christ, *Odes* 1:18: "Silence the made tambourines and the Berecynthian horn, of which the handmaids are blind self-love and vainglory, tossing an empty head too high."

If the merits of translations be weighed, it will be difficult to improve upon "sounding brass," but a bit more precision of connotation may be gained by "blaring horn" or "blaring brass." As for "clanging cymbal," this is an improvement over "tinkling cymbal," but "blatant cymbal" will be closer to the Greek, which suggests a vulgar bid for public attention.

Our understanding of still another verse may possibly be bettered if we keep this topic of self-love or egotism well in mind; and we shall be justified in so doing, because Paul is very tenacious of his topic. Let us then reconsider the words, "and though I have all faith, so that I could remove mountains." This can hardly mean faith in God, which is incompatible with egotism. It must rather mean faith in one's self, self-confidence. The reference will then be to boastful Homeric heroes, such as Ajax, who, having spent his weapons, seizes upon a huge rock, "such as two men would not avail to lift," and hurls it at his foe. This innuendo, obscured for us, would have been a schoolboy commonplace to Greeks. In their schools they memorized Homer, and the Homeric heroes were notorious for self-glorification.

Two notes of interest and importance remain to be recorded upon this topic of self-love. We still possess in extensive fragments a treatise by the Epicurean Philodemus of Gadara under the title of *Pride or Arrogance*, which is a synonym for the same vice. In this treatise he makes the significant observation that with the proud or arrogant man no cooperation is possible. That brotherly love, on the contrary, signifies sympathetic consideration for others and consequently renders feasible the working together that was to characterize each Christian group is made clear in verse 7, of which a new interpretation and translation will presently be offered.

Paul is here treading in the footsteps of Epicurus, as will be made clear by the second of the two notes that were promised. The treatise of Philodemus on *Pride or Arrogance* was the tenth book of his comprehensive study entitled *On Vices and the Corresponding Virtues*. How often Paul availed himself of this device of opposing the vice to the virtue has been abundantly demonstrated already. In this particular chapter he leads off by denouncing the vice of egotism or self-love before describing the virtue. When he comes to describe the virtue, he turns the Epicurean device of instruction into a trick of style, a most effective trick, which consists in defining the virtue by the vice, as in verses 4–5: "Love is patient and kind; love is *not* jealous or boastful; it is *not* arrogant or rude." No small part of the charm of this chapter as a devotional reading depends upon this adopted antithesis.

## Love Hopeth All Things

Conspicuous among the many merits of this hymn to love is a rhythm of phrasing that awakens in the subconscious mind the memory of certain psalms. The effect depends in the main upon the repetition of a given pattern of words, which may be observed at its best in the King James version of verse 7: "Beareth all things, believeth all things, hopeth all things, endureth all things." This charm is by no means accidental, because there is an unmistakable vein of poetry in Paul's disposition, and it may be said of his Epistles that, like the King James Version itself, they were "appointed to be read in churches." Nevertheless it may be added without hesitation that he stopped short of sacrificing the meaning for the sake of the sound, as if a light-minded poetaster or a shallow rhetorician.

It is consequently justifiable to ask ourselves what meaning really lies concealed beneath the gentle rhythm of this memorable verse. The meaning is certainly not on the surface, or if it is, we are no longer conditioned to apprehend it. What, then, would it have suggested to the Corinthians?

Our disability arises in part from the fact that we do not call love and friendship by the same name, as did both Epicurus and Paul. To Epicurus both were *philia*; to Paul both were *agape*.

Both words would have been familiar to Paul's readers in Corinth and both words would have signified friendship as well as love. If, then, we English readers can only divest ourselves of the habit of separating friendship from love, we shall have taken the first step toward recognizing in this seventh verse four qualities of true friendship according to the creed of Epicurus. It will be well to have the text before us: "Love beareth all things, believeth all things, hopeth all things, endureth all things."

A single searching glance will reveal that something is amiss. What is the difference, for example, between "beareth all things" and "endureth all things"? This is sheer tautology and Paul thinks too precisely and writes too precisely to be guilty of it. There must be an error of translation in one or the other. It turns out to be in the former. The Greek text does not read "beareth all things" but "keeps secret all things," or something similar. What this means, in turn, may readily be explained by recourse to Epicureanism.

To Epicurus love was friendship and friendship demanded loyalty. "Incorruptible loyalty" was the virtue chosen by the poet Horace to describe a deceased Epicurean friend. Moreover, men ought to feel gratitude for friendship and, according to Epicurus, "The wise man alone will feel true gratitude and in respect of his friends, *whether present or absent*, will be of the same mind throughout the journey of life." This means that the loyal friend will not belittle his friend behind his back or endure to hear him belittled. He will know his faults but will not be guilty of letting them become the topic of conversation with others.

Even more precision is possible. The members of each Epicurean group were committed to the practice of mutual admonition. They were to confide in one another. Paul fostered a like practice in his own churches, though he never seems to mention the virtue of confession so specifically as it is found in the Epistle of James, 5:16: "Confess your faults to one another." It is in his mind, however, and part of his meaning is that these confidences must be respected. It is for this reason that he writes: "Love keeps secret all things."

If, then, we aim at a version that will include both loyal silence concerning a friend's faults and loyal respect for faults confessed, we may suggest, "Love is always trustworthy." Defined by its opposite, the virtue may be worded, "Love never is false to a friend" or "Love never betrays a confidence."

The second phrase in verse 7, "believeth all things," is equally vague and obscure as we have it. This should rather be rendered, "Love is always trustful." This virtue is reciprocal to the former. Just as the true friend will always be loyal, so he will believe his friends to be worthy of loyalty. He will not be suspicious.

This topic of suspicion was a hackneyed one in ancient literature. Tyrants were notoriously distrustful of friends and would often ply them with wine in order to discover their real feelings. Hence the familiar saying, *in vino veritas*, that is, "Drunken men tell the truth." This trickery was specifically denounced by Epicurus; he is on record as saying that the wise man, who is to him the good man, "certainly will not watch men in their cups." He is also on record as repudiating the compulsory sharing of goods, "because that sort of thing was for those who did not trust one another, and if for such, it was not for friends."

It is the recognition of such teachings that demands the change from the obscure "believeth all things" to "Love is always trustful." Defined by its opposite, this means, "Love is never suspicious."

149

Just as love or friendship must be both trustworthy and trustful at all times, so it must also be hopeful, and this is the meaning of "hopeth all things." As made plain already in the foregoing chapter, in the ethic of Epicurus hopefulness is an attitude toward the future, deliberately chosen and pragmatically justified. It is assumed that the individual's experience can and must be controlled, the whole life must be rationally planned so as to ensure peace of mind and health of body, and this planning justifies the hope of pleasures to come.

This attitude is an essential of the happy life; not only is the individual the happier for being hopeful; he contributes also to the happiness of others. The virtue is social. So, instead of "Love hopeth all things," we may better read, "Love is always hopeful." Defining the virtue by its opposite, we may write: "Love is never pessimistic."

The last item in the list, "endureth all things," must, like the others, be interpreted in the sphere of human relations. We may be helped by knowledge of a running controversy between Epicureans and Stoics. The latter maintained that all offenses are equal; the man who steals a cabbage from his neighbor's garden is no less guilty than the man who robs a temple. The Epicureans, a charitable and forgiving sect, took a different view; they believed in making the punishment fit the crime.

Their attitude toward the trifling faults and frailties of their fellow men was similar. Epicurus himself laid stress upon the virtue that may be called considerateness; in his definition it approximates to the Golden Rule, though it falls short of recommending to turn the other cheek. Here are his words: "We value our own characters just as we do our private property, whether or not this be of the best and such as men would covet for themselves; in the same way we ought to have respect for the characters of others, if they are considerate."

This seems to be a rather novel way of looking at neighborly relations. Your neighbor's character, Epicurus seems to say, deserves to be treated with the same respect as his house. To modernize the application of this, if the mere thought of smashing a neighbor's windows would shame a man, why should not the thought of belittling his personality seem equally shameful? He may have his faults and defects. He may be extremely economical but this is no valid excuse for calling him Pinchpenny. His disposition may be unduly mild but this would not justify dubbing him Milquetoast. He may have a long visage but he need not be called Horseface. He may talk too much but this would not excuse the gibe of Gabby Jones. Have we no faults or defects ourselves? Forbearance should be mutual.

Therefore, instead of "Love endureth all things," we may more correctly read, "Love is always tolerant." The negative version will be, "Love is never censorious."

The whole verse may now be rendered with more precision than before: "Love is always trustworthy, always trustful, always hopeful, always tolerant." The negative versions will run: "Love is never treacherous, never suspicious, never pessimistic, never censorious."

## Interim and Recognition

At this point it will be profitable to pause and take a second and more discerning glance over the structure of this fascinating chapter. From the Hebrew point of view it seems to be a psalm of love; it exhibits a rhythm of language that harmonizes aptly with the rhythm of thought; one sentiment follows another like gentle waves lapping upon a beach, after the fashion of the twenty-third psalm.

At the same time we catch the glimmer of Greek philosophy. When we read, "Rejoiceth not in iniquity, but rejoiceth in the truth," this must be recognized as the Epicurean device of instruction, employed here as a trick of style, again opposing "the vice to the corresponding virtue."

From another point of view this chapter may with equal propriety be regarded as an ode to love in the Greek manner. The Greek ode exhibits a definite pattern of arrangement. The thought moves lightly from one aspect to another of a single theme, following a chosen association of ideas, which may conceal a genuine logic.

Such is the procedure here. The first aspect of love is the ugly one, egotism or self-love, which blows its own horn and beats the drum of its own fame. Next come the dual aspects of love, the virtues defined by the vices. Last comes the summary in verse 7, four aspects of true brotherly love or friendship.

The rest of this hybrid of poetical invention, psalm of love or ode to love, verses 8–13, presents new aspects of the pervading theme, which cannot be understood unless the assumptions that underlie them have been detected and rendered explicit. These assumptions have been obscured for the modern reader by the ruthless march of time, although to ancient readers they were the veriest commonplace.

## Interim

The first of these assumptions may be called the idea of the interim, by which is signified Paul's conviction that the generation to which he belonged was living under temporary conditions. The termination of this interim was to be marked by the second coming of Christ, the signal for the general resurrection. The prior limit of the interim was the resurrection of Christ himself. Thus Paul's generation was thought to be living in the interim of time between the two resurrections.

It may go without saying that this notion of an interim was not original with Paul but in one form or another had been a component of public thought from a date long before this time.

We should find the history of the idea both interesting and profitable. For the purpose of detecting its origin a principle espoused by Epicurus himself may prove useful. It was his contention that Nature, the sole creatrix, manifests herself in the cumulative experience of each race and in the aggregate experience of mankind. History is thus the evolution of the unintended. This implies that actions always precede words and events precede ideas.

To apply this principle to the notion of the interim, the event that preceded and was the cause of it was the downfall of the kingdom in Israel. The reaction of the Hebrew prophets to this event was to predict the restoration of the kingdom and to this end a divine king must come with supernatural power, that is, the Messiah.

Such, then, was the origin of the notion of the interim; in its original form it was the space of time between the downfall of the kingdom and the expected restoration. It manifested itself in the public mind as a sense of temporariness in things, sometimes contemplated with fear and despair, sometimes with ardent hope. The speed with which it took possession of the mind of Israel is not astonishing, because the mass opinion of the race had long been shaped to a major degree by prophecy; but the rapidity with which it extended itself to neighboring peoples is truly astounding. The savior sentiment became a universal component of the public imagination.

The sense of temporariness and expectancy imparted a tremendous impulse to the arts of prophecy. The picayune predictions of Apollo were suddenly outmoded and his very name became obscured in the growing popularity of his own priestesses, the Sibyllae, who began to chart the future in the grander style of the Hebrews. Their language alone was Greek.

Astrology also sprang to sudden popularity and swept rapidly from east to west. The comet that appeared after the murder of Julius Caesar gave a smart fillip to the notion of the savior star. The star, the Sibyl, and the divine child were all celebrated in the poetry of Virgil before the birth of Christ. The glamour of these oriental ideas attached itself to the name of Caesar, the more readily because the Romans themselves, long plagued by civil wars, had become conscious of living in an interim of time. It should not be astonishing, therefore, that when order seemed to have been restored at last, a superstitious senate conferred upon the younger Caesar the title of Augustus, which is as close as the Latin language can approach to the idea of "the anointed one."

Having clearly apprehended this notion of the interim, we can now discern a serious mistranslation in the last verse of this challenging chapter, "but the greatest of these is love." Paul reasons precisely and writes precisely and we ought to translate him precisely. It is not the superlative degree of the adjective that he here employs but the comparative, and what he writes means "but love ranks higher than these." He does not tell us but leaves it to us to discern that faith and hope are not of the nature of God himself but belong exclusively to human experience. They are virtues of the interim and being such will terminate, while love, being of the nature of God himself, will never end. It is for this reason that love ranks higher.

The correction of the translation, however, must await a fuller discussion of the notion of the interim.

## Knowledge and the Interim

We must next observe that belief in the interim reacts also upon the thinker's conception of knowledge. Epicurus, for example, believing as he did that mortal life is an interim between two eternities of unconsciousness, was bound also to assume that the only kind of knowledge is that which characterizes the interim of mortal life. There was nothing in consequence to deter him from judging his own system of knowledge to be perfect, which he did; he called it "true reason" or "true philosophy" or simply "truth" and his disciples boasted of their devotion to this "truth."

Paul, with his usual acumen, pounced upon this assumption of perfection and proceeded to belittle it as a fallacy. Believing as he did in the temporariness of things, he was bound to believe also in two kinds of knowledge, the one of the interim and imperfect, the other of eternity and perfect. From this it followed by cogent inference that the philosophy of Epicurus must be of this transitory world and by virtue of this fact imperfect.

## When I Was a Child

If this argument commends itself as a shrewd one, it still falls short of revealing the full measure of Paul's acumen. He casually presses the same logic to another notch and denominates the philosophy of Epicurus as doubly inferior, first, because it is of this temporary world and consequently imperfect, and second, because it is typical of the shorter interim of human life that we call adolescence and consequently juvenile.

It may, of course, seem to be a sort of vandalism to seize upon this gem of diction out of the King James Bible, the verse that begins "When I was a child, I spake as a child," jettison all the pensive sentiment it inevitably evokes, and discern beneath the pensiveness, which we falsely read into it, a biting specimen of logical satire; but, if our quest be the discovery of Paul's meaning and if this quest is not to be relinquished, then as satire it must be identified. It may even happen that a new and worthier pensiveness may be restored to it.

Already in the study of Galatians 4:3 we have discovered the use of the word *child* to be an error of translation. The Greek word, it is true, means an infant in the sense that English law regards all individuals short of legal age as infants; but the word has connotations outside of law. To Paul it denotes one who has not yet arrived at the age of discretion, mental maturity. So in Galatians 4:3 we have emended the translation to read: "When we were juveniles, we were slaves to the elements of the universe." This means that in the interim of adolescence we were captivated by the philosophy of Epicurus.

If by this time we have achieved willingness to sacrifice an exquisite specimen of simple diction for the sake of the real meaning, verse 11 may be paraphrased as follows: "When I was a sophomore, I used to indulge in reckless talk, the way sophomores do; I used to entertain wild ideas, the way sophomores do; I used to startle people with smart arguments, the way sophomores do. When I became a real adult person, I made an end of such antics."

The reference, overt to ancient readers though covert to us, is to the Epicureans. Paul is mocking the mockers, tossing back from his own trench a grenade of their throwing. It was their pleasure to ridicule the idea of the resurrection as silliness; it was his pleasure to damn their brand of knowledge as typical of the folly of adolescence. In his view of things the interim of time in which his generation was living was bound to be characterized by imperfection of knowledge but the creed of Epicurus was of a quality much lower; it was excusable only as the irresponsible thinking of the smaller interim of adolescence, something that was part of the process of growing up but due to be outgrown.

Having improved our understanding of this verse by a paraphrase, perhaps we may gain further benefit by a sort of parody, dilating the innocent language of the King James Version to admit authenticated items of Epicurean doctrine, such as Paul detested: "The age of adolescence will talk recklessly as if the only things that are not seen are beggarly specks of matter called atoms; it will have wild ideas as if God lived aloof to the affairs of mankind; it will shock pious people by adducing reasons for believing that the world was no more created for the sake of man than for the sake of beetles."

## Now We See in a Mirror, Indistinctly

Having thoroughly discounted the philosophy of materialism by an innuendo perspicuous at the time, though for us understandable only by paraphrase and parody, Paul resumes his theme with a variation, as befits the author of an ode. Neither is it unbefitting that this variation is a figure of speech, slightly obscure for us, though less so than the innuendo that precedes. The ancients knew only mirrors of bronze, darker than brass at best, and usually tarnished. So we should read: "Now we see in a mirror, indistinctly, but then face to face."

To us modern readers this seemingly innocent verse may be an invitation to relaxation of mind and the contemplative mood, but in reality it is packed with meaning and should be challenging to the attention. Individual words will be found to repay separate scrutiny, and hints will be uncovered of the unexpressed assumptions of Paul's thought and also of the public mind of his time. An immediate reward will be the promised correction of the translation, though additional dividends of value will also accrue.

When Paul writes "Now we see," his specific reference is to the temporary conditions of the interim of time in which he believed his own generation to be living, awaiting the second coming; when in the next verse he writes "Now I know in part," the reference is the same. When he writes "but then I shall know," the reference is to the occasion of the second coming and its glorious sequels.

The mistranslation comes in the last verse, which by the King James Version is made to begin, "And now abideth faith, hope, charity," and by the Revised Standard, "So faith, hope, love abide." What has been overlooked is the fact that Paul has switched from a casual Greek word meaning "now" to an emphatic synonym, which may be rendered "as things now are." This correction enables us to detect and correct a second error, which lies in "abideth" or "abide." As already pointed out, faith and hope differ from love in being virtues of the interim, which terminates at the second coming, while love is eternal, being of the nature of God himself. A precise version will then read: "But as things now are, faith, hope, love remain valid, these three, but love ranks higher than these two." Faith and hope are appointed to lose validity but not love.

## The Concept of Recognition

The next step for us is to follow up a second clue of thought, which has lain unobserved in the verse that mentions the mirror. The key words are "indistinctly, but then face to face," which presume a concept of recognition that was part of the popular psychology of Paul's time. If this concept shall seem strange to us, there is all the more reason for the effort to become familiar with it; Paul's reasoning will be found to hinge upon it.

To begin at the beginning is a sound plan of procedure, even at the risk of being tedious, and this brings us back to Epicurus. In the world of Paul he occupied a position not unlike that of Sigmund Freud in our own day. Freud, though infinitely irritating, has captured the public attention. Epicurus succeeded in holding the attention of the ancient world for seven centuries, irritating men over the whole period. In the fourth century the Christian Lactantius was still smarting over Epicurean ridicule of "the wrath of God," though at the same time con-

ceding that the disciples of Epicurus had always outnumbered the adherents of other sects.

If in the fourth century it was still impossible for Lactantius to
ignore Epicureanism, then on the wane, in the first century it was infinitely more impossible for Paul to ignore it, because it was already
popular and widely diffused and still on the increase. It was well publicized in handy texts, which were often revised. Among these was a
standard handbook entitled *On the Sensations*, the work of Metrodorus.
From this book and basic writings of Epicurus himself were derived
certain notions of psychology which then prevailed. These enjoyed
the greater vogue because the Stoics, always apt at imitating success,
assisted in the work of popularizing them.

We can make immediate progress by becoming acquainted with a
specimen of Epicurean psychology. The textbooks have perished but
sufficient evidences survive for the reconstruction of a sample lecture.

Let us assume that the observer discerns something white moving in
the distance in the twilight. It may be a white ox or it may be a human
being dressed in white. It comes nearer; it is recognized to be a human
figure. It may be a man or it may be a woman. It comes still nearer; it
is seen to be a man. It continues to come nearer; it is seen to be bearded.
As it draws closer it is seen to walk with the shoulders slightly stooped.
At last it comes into plain view; the observer recognizes the man and
exclaims, "It is Plato."

Now this exposition, which must needs be made so very explicit for
the modern man, would have been for intelligent readers of Paul's time
the sheerest commonplace. They would have been familiar, for instance, with the principles illustrated in this synthetic lecture: first, the
particulars or parts are discerned in advance of the whole; second, the
act of recognition is a synthesis of the parts or particulars; and third,
only the immediate sensation is dependable — it alone results in a definite recognition.

Such is the concept of recognition in its simplest form; to allow it to
grow in our minds will be a revealing experience, because it exhibits
various aspects.

In the meanwhile, what is the application of it? What are we to read
out of it? We are to read this, that Paul employs the then familiar terminology and ideology of sensation in order to explain things that lie
beyond the range of sensation. We are catching him in the very act of

making himself "as a Greek to the Greeks," drawing upon the resources of philosophy to build his structure of religion.

Epicurus divided all existing things into two classes: those that lie within the range of sensation and those that lie beyond the range of sensation. This may be paraphrased as the seen and the unseen, the visible and the invisible. Paul takes over this division of things, employing the very same words, *orata, aorata,* which no other writer employs in the New Testament. Yet what a difference of application! To Epicurus the invisible things, too minute to be discerned by the physical eye, are the atoms, which are eternal. To Paul the invisible things are spiritual, God himself, for example, who is eternal.

In this quest it is vital to observe that the knowledge of spiritual things, and the knowledge of God in particular, is arrived at through an experience of recognition no less than knowledge of physical things, including human beings. In fact there is no choice open to Paul but to employ the terminology of physical sensation to describe the spiritual experience. It should be recalled that only when the approaching figure has come close can the observer say, "It is Plato."

So in Paul's verse, "Now we see in a mirror, indistinctly, but then face to face," the "face to face" recognition will be final and decisive. It is just as if the living man, caught up in glory on the last day, should exclaim, "This is God!" Yet this event, even if comparable to a blinding physical experience, will be much more; it will also be a spiritual experience. It will be a final realization of the nature of God. It will be an experience of recognition.

## Aspects of Recognition

After this anticipatory glance over the topic of recognition we shall profit by attempting a closer scrutiny. It exhibits various aspects. It is essentially an experience of discovery and operates on all levels of learning, whether sensory, rational, or spiritual. On the sensory level we recognize a person; this is a discovery of identity only; it answers the question "Who is it?" On the rational level we recognize, for example, that Paul has a double ethic, one of the interim and destined to terminate at the resurrection, the other permanent. This is an experience of the mind. On the spiritual level, although we still employ the terminology of sensory experience, the question is no longer "Who is it?"

but rather "What is he like?" or "What is his true nature?" and the answer is found in First John 3:2: "We shall see him as he is."

Certain special aspects of recognition will next claim our attention. When we recognize the identity of a person on the street, this is an involuntary act, and we recognize many with whom we have no personal acquaintance. In the case of those people who are personal friends or acquaintances we may or may not choose to recognize them by a greeting or gesture, because this act is voluntary and quite distinct from the involuntary recognition of identity.

We are now approaching something important. The act of recognition may be elevated to the rank of a ritual or a formality. For example, the President of the United States on the advice of his Cabinet may concede or withhold the recognition of a foreign power. If recognition is conceded, the representative of such country is received at the White House and welcomed to the circle of foreign ministers.

The importance of this aspect of recognition lies in the fact that it is part of Paul's mind and unless we apprehend it ourselves we shall misunderstand what Paul writes and also mistranslate it. An example of this error may be found in First Corinthians 15:34, where the Revised Standard reads: "For some have no knowledge of God. I say this to your shame."

If some people have no knowledge of God because they were never told about him, this is no reason for shame but rather for pity. In point of fact, the question in this instance is not a matter of knowledge at all but rather of recognition; the people concerned have been told about God and still refuse recognition, which is an affront to God. Hence the shame. It is an insult just as the refusal of an individual to recognize his superior or the refusal of one government to recognize another is an insult.

If Paul's words in the above verse be closely scrutinized in the Greek, we shall discover that he is not merely stating a fact but resorting to an idiom of characterization. He is informing the Corinthians of a group among them who know about God but are so shameless as to offer him affront by refusing to recognize him. In Paul's language, to know God has a technical meaning; no other means of entering upon this knowledge exists except to recognize God by recognizing the resurrected Christ. The word *recognition* is also technical in force and virtually indispensable. Hence we may translate: "For some among you are refusing recognition to God. I say this to your shame."

## Mutual Recognition

Still other aspects of recognition await exploration. The believer's experience of God, which is begun by his recognition of the Son of God in the person of the resurrected Christ, is not one-sided but reciprocal. At the same moment that the individual recognizes the Son he is recognized by the Father. This detail of doctrine finds its confirmation in Galatians 4:9: "but now that you have come to know God, or rather to be known by God." This verse not only demonstrates the reciprocal nature of the experience but also contains the fruitful hint that the recognition of the individual by God is the more significant part of the said experience. This aspect of the recognition, however, must await its turn elsewhere.

Another verse that possesses bearing upon the mutual or reciprocal nature of recognition is found in First Corinthians 8:3: "But if one loves God, he is known by him." This is one of many instances where Paul's reasoning is highly syncopated. It is here plainly implied, though not expressly stated, that knowledge does not constitute a valid bid for recognition by God. It "puffs up" but has no promise of things to come. It is the love of the individual for God that qualifies the individual for recognition by God and contains the promise of growth to come.

Elsewhere, however, it is the profession of faith in the resurrected Christ that constitutes the valid claim for recognition by God. By what reasoning, then, can love be substituted for faith? The answer may be found in Galatians 5:6, if correctly translated; faith must be activated by love. Love, in a sense, is faith at work. If a man really loves God, he will also love his neighbor and refrain from causing him to do wrong, for example, by eating meat sacrificed to idols. By this practical demonstration of brotherly love he will qualify for recognition by God and "be known by God."

In order to explore the next aspect of recognition we must recall the doctrine of Epicurus which asserted the total indifference of the gods toward human wickedness. Reciprocal to this was his teaching that these same gods were not indifferent toward the pious. His words are worth quoting, not only for their intrinsic importance but also because they occur in his letter addressed to a lad Menoeceus, a minor gem of

160

Greek literature, which Paul himself gives evidence of having known at first hand: "[The gods] being exclusively concerned with their own virtues, are receptive toward those like themselves, deeming all that is not such as alien." By their own virtues he means chiefly tranquillity, unruffled calm, and it was even his teaching that human beings who enjoy such peace of mind may be visited by filmy images of the gods, too subtle to be apprehended by the eyes of the flesh but capable of being perceived by the mind.

The significance to be observed in this teaching is the implied suggestion of the recognition of the pious by the gods. Philodemus was slightly more specific in declaring that "the gods are friends of the wise and the wise are friends of the gods." The concept of recognition, however, failed to click and this in spite of the fact that it was well understood in Epicurean psychology.

It was Paul who seized upon this concept and elaborated it with explicitness, and we may be prepared to discover other coincidences in his new pattern of thought. Even the Epicurean doctrine of the indifference of the gods toward the wicked will have its analogue.

There was no concept of recognition in Jewish religious thought. If we scan the Wisdom Literature, especially Psalms and Proverbs, where individuality and ethical inwardness in religious experience first become plainly manifest, all men, good or bad, are individuals in the sight of God. He may look upon the wicked with disfavor but he is by no means unaware of their identity. He is displeased with them or even angry at them as individuals.

Paul the innovator had no hesitation in rejecting this easy and informal attitude. He institutes a new and specific qualification for the divine favor, the profession of faith in the resurrected Christ. Mankind is no longer divided into the righteous and the wicked, both of them alike being individuals in God's sight; the new division is into believers and unbelievers. The former are recognized by God and become individuals in his sight; upon the latter God turns his back — they become a nameless multitude without individuality. We find Paul's teaching on this question in the first chapter of Romans, especially verse 28, of which the translation in the Revised Standard leaves much to be desired: "And since they did not see fit to acknowledge God, God gave them up to a base mind and to improper conduct."

The cardinal error in this translation is to dispense with the word *recognition*; this is technical and will not admit of a substitute. It is a mistake also to overlook an idiom of characterization over and above the statement of fact; Paul is not only stating what these men did but also what kind of men they were. So we may tentatively translate: "And since they disapproved of vouchsafing recognition to God, God abandoned them to their reprobate minds and to go on with their sins."

This doctrine becomes highly astonishing when we observe how closely Paul is approaching the position of Epicurus. The declaration of the latter that the gods regarded all who were not like themselves as "alien" should be recalled. How better could this adjective *alien* be amplified than to say with Paul that "God abandoned them to their reprobate minds and to go on with their sins"? In other words, the wicked have become to God, as they were to the gods of Epicurus, a nameless multitude, with no more individuality than sheep.

Yet this parallelism of doctrine does not stand alone. God is no longer ordaining any temporal punishment for wickedness. He is thus relieved of his duties as an officer of law enforcement, which Epicurus ridiculed as demeaning to the sanctity of the divine being. Neither is any punishment for wickedness put in prospect for the world to come. Thus Hell is abolished just as it was abolished by Epicurus. There is a difference, however; God is still a god of wrath and the penalty appointed for the wicked is annihilation at the last day.

## The Bid for Recognition

Now at last it becomes possible to integrate neatly the concept of recognition into Paul's new structure of doctrine. This concept becomes reciprocal to God's abandonment of unbelievers to their reprobate minds and continuance of sin. If God had not assumed this attitude, no necessity would have arisen for the individual to make a bid for recognition by God.

The individual must make the first move. He must recognize Jesus as the Son of God in the person of the resurrected Christ. This is his bid for recognition by God the Father, who instantly reciprocates by recognizing him. At that moment he ceases to be one of a multitude devoid of individuality and becomes an individual with a name, Dionysius the Areopagite or Lydia the seller of purple or whatever the name may be. Thereafter the relationship between him and God is personal. The individual becomes a person in the sight of God and God to him a person. This is what Paul means by "knowing God" or "being known by God."

Yet even if a higher degree of precision seems to have been here achieved, we must not be content. Our understanding will be further improved by observing subsidiary aspects of this mutual recognition between man and God. To this end we may once more quote Galatians 4:9: "now that you have come to know God, or rather to be known of God." These words, while making clear beyond doubt the reciprocal nature of the experience, suggest also the inequality of the experience. The best that the individual can do is to afford pleasure to God but God is capable of making a richer return; he can furnish inspiration, guidance, and strength to the believer. It is consequently a temptation to emend the translation and read: "now that you have come to know God or, *better still*, to be known by God." The individual enters upon a new life, the life of the Spirit, which is eternal.

A second inequality in this mutual recognition now awaits notice and examination. In the Greek as Paul uses it, "knowledge" is *gnosis* and "recognition" is *epignosis*. With God himself these two words are synonymous. His first recognition of the individual is knowledge of the individual; it is perfect from the first. This is not true for the individual. His first recognition of God is only the beginning of knowledge of God. This knowledge is imperfect, even if progressive, and throughout the whole interim of life in the flesh will continue to be imperfect. Fullness of knowledge must await a final experience of recognition.

## The Final Recognition

We are now at last equipped to scrutinize anew and interpret and translate the difficult twelfth verse of this thirteenth chapter. The words "face to face" remind us definitely that we have the phenomenon of recognition to deal with. Only the immediate sensation, as Epicurus taught, is true and dependable; the distant views fall short of exactitude. A hackneyed example in ancient times was that of the square tower, which in the distance appears to be round. Only the near view reveals its real shape.

When once we have accepted the idea that this way of reasoning was commonplace in Paul's time, just as explaining human conduct by means of inferiority complexes and other inward compulsions is characteristic of the public mind today, we shall better understand why he expresses spiritual experiences in terms of sensory experiences. He may well have been influenced also by the revelation that came to him on the way to Damascus, which was at one and the same time a blinding physical experience and an explosive spiritual experience, a genuine experience of recognition, the breaking of a new horizon of understanding.

Perhaps no better way of arriving at the best possible degree of precision may be found than by putting the King James translation of verse 12 to the test: "Now I know in part; but then I shall know even as also I am known." This wording exhibits the deceptive smoothness that constitutes a merit for devotional readings but misses utterly the essentials of meaning. Paul is not setting side by side two kinds of knowledge but two distinct experiences of recognition. His language is virtually technical.

First of all, we must have respect for tenses. The recognition of the individual by God was a distinct and instantaneous event in the past. Therefore, instead of "even as also I am known" we should read "even as also I became known." In other words, in the experience of God himself there is no such thing as an interim; in his experience the first recognition was perfect from the first. In the experience of the individual, on the contrary, the first recognition marks the beginning of an interim; this recognition is imperfect, even if progressive. Perfection of knowledge must await an event in the future, the final recognition, which will be instantaneous, like the previous recognition by God, and will terminate the interim.

The authors of the Revised Standard have endeavored to improve upon the King James but fall into the same inaccuracies: "then I shall understand fully, even as I have been fully understood." The insertion of the word *fully*, because it is implied in the context, has a certain justification; but even so, instead of "even as I have been fully understood" we should read "even as I became fully understood," because God's recognition of the individual was an event in the past, single, distinct, perfect, and final.

The vital defect of both versions, however, is their flatness. There is nothing in the wording to suggest the miraculous character of the anticipated experience as hinted in Philippians 3:21, when the lowly body of the believer will be changed "to be like his glorious body"; and still less are we prompted to think of the miracle of the victory over death in First Corinthians 15:52, when "the trumpet shall sound, and the dead shall be raised incorruptible, and we shall be changed."

Paul is a man of visions and he cannot but think of the religious experience in terms of vivid sensory experiences, vivid even to the degree of explosiveness. It is this bent of his mind that makes him so partial to the word *recognition* and the concept behind it. He takes this over from the public thought of his day but he extends it to meet the necessities of his own structure of doctrine. The experience of the resurrection is inevitably prefigured in terms of his own explosive experience on the road to Damascus.

If we consult the account of that experience in the lucid words of the ninth chapter of Acts, we shall find it to begin with the words, "and suddenly a light from heaven flashed about him." It was in light that Jesus manifested himself to him. The use of the word *light* is an obsession with Paul. He thinks of the gospel, of immortality, of heaven, of Jesus, of God, and of the resurrection all in terms of light.

It is characteristic of the phenomenon of recognition that it comes with a flash. This is true even in so ordinary an experience as the recognition of a person, though more noticeably so when a person has not been seen for a long time and recognition is delayed; at the last it is an instantaneous phenomenon. It is also a pleasure.

Magnify this experience to the utmost limits of the imagination and we shall descry Paul's conception of the believer's final recognition of the nature of God as we read it in First Corinthians 13:12. It will come with a burst of light, an ecstatic transition from imperfect knowledge to perfect knowledge, a dazzling visual illumination. In a moment, in the twinkling of an eye, he will come to know God, just as he became known to God.

Translation is difficult but the obligation to attempt it is mandatory. Paul's ten words are precise, compacted, and virtually technical. He does not write: "I shall know even as I was known," but literally, "I shall recognize even as I too was recognized." It is this phenomenon of recognition that cannot be ignored, an instantaneous phenomenon. Reluctantly we suggest: "Now I know in part, but in that day knowledge will come to me in a flash, just as I too became known."

A last note is due on the phenomenon of recognition. No less in literature than in ancient philosophy and psychology it played a leading role, especially when the effect was heightened by suspense and surprise. In the drama the most gripping of all scenes were those in which a concealed identity was revealed at last, as when Oedipus was discovered by his own research to have been the murderer of his own father. In the whole of the Greek drama, however, no recognition scene can be found which for concentrated power of passion and surprise is the superior of that described in the unpretentious narrative of Luke, Acts 9:1–9, where Paul, prostrate and blinded, hears the words from heaven: "I am Jesus, whom thou persecutest."

Here in the brief space of a single paragraph we have before us in unique combination the highest essentials of the tragic drama and no less the kindred religious experience of spiritual discovery and illumination.

# ❖ X ❖

# PAUL'S KNOWLEDGE OF EPICUREANISM

Iᴛ sᴛɪʟʟ remains for us to scrutinize some evidences of Paul's
knowledge of Epicureanism which do not fall within the scope of particular Epistles. By way of preparation for this scrutiny, however, it
will be well for us to cast a sweeping glance at the factors of history
and geography, subscribing for the moment to the view of Epicurus
that all events are "accidents of time, place, and persons." We shall also
better our understanding by recognizing to what extent the success of
Paul's ministries depended upon the high level of education which was
prevailing during his time.

The first phenomenon that calls for our attention is the vast shifts of
population that took place in the three centuries that intervened between the lifetime of Epicurus and that of Paul. It was an era of great
migrations.

The first migration was that of Greeks into the East to build and
populate the hundreds of new cities founded by Alexander the Great
and his successors. This exploitation was accomplished with astonishing
speed, only to be followed quickly by the political confusion that regularly characterized Greek affairs. It was this confusion that provoked
and justified conquest by the steadier genius of Rome. After this conquest a contrary movement of population set in toward the West and
to Italy in particular.

Both of these migrations were accompanied by the philosophy of
Epicurus. It was already flourishing, for example, in Tarsus and Antioch in the second century B.C. but did not flourish in Rome until the
following century in the lifetime of Julius Caesar and Cicero.

Corresponding to these mass migrations of Greeks there were mass
migrations of Jews in the opposite direction. A replacement of popula-

167

tions was taking place. As the Greeks swarmed eastward into the Near East and beyond, the Jews began to move northward and westward into Asia Minor, Macedonia, and the mainland of Greece. These migrations of Jews, the so-called Diaspora, were followed in their turn by Christianity.

The pattern of all these movements, both the migrations that preceded and the cultural changes that followed in their wakes, is typified in the person and activities of Paul. He was a Jew by birth, by early education an Epicurean, and by conversion a Christian. He began his ministry in Syria and Cilicia, spent the greater part of his life among the mixed populations of Jews and Greeks in Asia Minor, Macedonia, and the mainland of Greece, and last of all arrived in Rome, the ultimate goal and limit of the influences of the East.

## Philosophy, Religion, and Education

So much for migrations and countermigrations and their cultural sequels. The second requisite for gaining the synoptic view of events is to observe to what extent these cultural sequels depended upon the existence of a literate public.

The philosophy of Epicurus depended to a special degree upon the literacy of Greek and other populations. Its creed was embodied from the first in handy textbooks, compiled with a special view to home study and group study. Its appeal was not to princes and the friends of princes, as in the case of Platonism, but rather to the intelligent and educated middle class. Its method of extension was from friend to friend. Each disciple delighted to carry the handbooks of Epicurus in his wallet and pass them to others for reading. Moreover, these textbooks were graded in such a way as to encourage more and more reading. Once begun, the course of study was believed to result in a sequence of revelation.

The student was encouraged to be self-dependent in his reading; he was compared to a hound that had been set upon the trail: "Thus by your own efforts you will be able to spot one clue after another, work your way into all the dark recesses, and drag forth the truth to light." Pauline Christianity, of course, was equally dependent upon the existence of a literate public. Paul was not following the example of Jesus, who wrote nothing, shunned the cities, sought out the lost sheep in byways, villages, and mountains, and spoke in parables. Paul, a product of urban life and education, heads invariably for the towns and cities, and most of his Epistles are specifically addressed to the inhabitants of cities.

It is possible to say more: Paul's public was not only intelligent and literate; it was well-to-do, and this was especially true of the Philippians. For instance, he writes in Second Corinthians 11:9: "During my sojourn with you, when I ran short, I did not sponge on anyone, because the friends who had come from Macedonia made up my deficiency and more." Again in Philippians 4:14–19 we find him embarrassed by the generosity of that church. This generosity occasioned him another kind of embarrassment, because it gave to some the excuse for accusing him of using his apostleship for gain, against which he defends himself by boasting of his sufferings. It was the same calumny of jealous rivals that caused him to make a point of working with his hands.

The vast difference between the cultural level of those to whom Paul addressed himself and that of those classes sought out by other preachers is vividly presented by a testimony of the churchman Origen, who quotes a hostile critic. This critic accuses the Christians of putting a discount upon education.

"Otherwise," he demands to know, "why is it a demerit to have received an education and to be intelligent and to be thought so? Why should this disqualify one from arriving at a knowledge of God? Why should it not rather be a prerequisite and something by virtue of which a man might better arrive at a grasp of the truth? But what we actually see is this, that those who collect an audience and ventilate the wildest ideas in the market places will never go near a group of intelligent men nor drum up their courage to air their doctrines in the presence of such; but whenever they espy some teen-age lads or a bevy of household slaves or a throng of empty-headed individuals, there they push their way in and strut their stuff."

Whatever discount we may place upon this diatribe, it still may be useful in compelling us to realize how superior was the intelligence and education of those to whom Paul addressed himself. In First Corinthians 3:2 he chided his readers for being "babes in Christ," fit to be fed with milk and not solid food, but in the very first chapter of this Epistle he assumed that these readers would understand his irony in dubbing the atoms of Epicurus "the things that are" and spiritual realities "the things that are not." In the second chapter of this same Epistle he assumes that his readers understand the meaning of a criterion of truth; and he sets up a new criterion, paying those readers the high compliment of employing language fit to be tested by the precision gauge of logic: "The spiritual man judges all things, but is himself to be judged by no one."

Paul further presumes upon the intelligence and education of his readers by the drastic condensation of argument. He seems to have shared the fear of verbosity with Epicurus, one of whose warnings runs: "We must realize that the long discourse and the short discourse aim at the same objective." Paul's addiction to the short discourse may even seem to have been carried to extremes. For instance, when he writes that "the spiritual man judges all things," he may seem to claim too much. Certainly he would not have us believe that spiritual insight is a judge of colors, nor that it operates on the sensory level at all, nor even on the rational level of thought. What he really did mean is stated with curt exactitude in verse 11: "For what person knows a man's thoughts except the spirit of the man which is in him? So also no one understands the thoughts of God except the Spirit of God."

The validity of the new criterion is confined to a definite level of experience; it is an insight into human personality and the nature of God.

## On the Nature of Things

There is still more to be gleaned, however, from Paul's assumptions. These not only enlighten us upon the high degree of intelligence and education which he presumed in his readers, but also inform us of the extent of his own knowledge of Epicureanism.

One of the first writings of Epicurus was an encyclopedic work in thirty-seven rolls entitled *On the Nature of Things*. This would have made a volume of perhaps fifteen hundred pages if printed in the type and format of the Revised Standard New Testament. It was speedily supplemented by what came to be called the Big Epitome, in seven rolls, which would make a book of half the size of the Revised Standard New Testament. This Epitome was supplemented in turn by a Little Epitome, which is still extant as a letter addressed to Herodotus. It runs to twenty-five pages of text.

Thus we have the titles of three writings of Epicurus covering the same ground but we are able to identify the level of knowledge presumed by Paul in his readers as corresponding to the Big Epitome. We are able to infer this because we know that Epicurus set up three criteria of truth, Sensations, Feelings, and Anticipations, and of these only the Sensations find mention in Paul's Epistles, as in Colossians 2:18: "taking his stand on what he has seen, puffed up without justification by the mind of the flesh." This is precisely what we find in the poem of the Roman poet Lucretius, who reproduced in Latin the Big Epitome; he dwells upon the Sensations as criteria but offers no exposition of the other two. There is another item of evidence pointing in the same direction. When Paul in the verse quoted above speaks of "the mind of the flesh," this refers plainly to the doctrine of Epicurus that the mind is an organ of the body no less than the eyes or the ears, which is emphasized by Lucretius while not explicitly stated in the Little Epitome.

Neither the Big nor the Little Epitome of Epicurus deals specifically with the subject of ethics but they make it abundantly clear that the source of ethical principles is to be found in the physical principles. In other words, Nature is the supreme teacher. Paul reveals his awareness of this doctrine by the vehemence with which he asserts the substitute doctrine that "all the treasures of wisdom and knowledge" are hidden in God. Yet his youthful allegiance to the creed of Epicurus so far prevails over the convictions of his mature age that he finds it quite easy to write "according to nature" and "contrary to nature" and in First Corinthians 11:14 actually recognizes the principle he elsewhere repudiates: "Does not Nature herself teach you?" This phraseology is foreign to the New Testament except in his Epistles. In spite of himself he shares the Epicurean slant of the public mind of the time.

There is one doctrine, however, in respect of which Paul is never off his guard, the teaching that pleasure is the end or the goal of living and sanctioned by Nature as such. The roll in which this doctrine was expounded bore the title *On the End* and its celebrity was unsurpassed, because it was beloved by disciples and abhorred by enemies. This abhorrence is shared by Paul, in spite of the fact that he must have known the innocence of the word *pleasure* as employed by Epicurus, who wrote: "Whenever we say pleasure is the end, we do not mean the pleasures of profligates and those pleasures that consist in self-indulgence, but the absence of pain in the body and of turmoil in the soul."

In Paul's thinking the mere mention of the word *pleasure* is hazardous and he studiously avoids it, using it but once and then in an evil sense, Titus 3:3. The studious avoidance, however, reveals his awareness of the dangerous ambiguity of the doctrine for which the word stood. His silence points to his fears; no compromise with pleasure was conceivable.

The second ethical writing of Epicurus that ranked as a classic was entitled *On Choices and Avoidances* but for Paul this seems to have been superseded by the later work of Philodemus of Gadara entitled *On Vices and the Corresponding Virtues,* several times cited in previous chapters. The influence of this treatise is ubiquitous in Paul's writing, sometimes as an effective device of style, as in First Corinthians 13, but more often, as with the Epicureans, a device of instruction, especially in Galatians 5:19–24, where "the works of the flesh" are summed up in a prodigious list of vices as opposed to "the fruit of the Spirit." Similar lists have been called to attention in Colossians 3:1–8, where earthly things are set in opposition to "things that are above." The appeal of this device to the modern mind is attested by the popularity of these passages as devotional readings.

Other devotional readings that find favor with modern congregations and can be traced to an Epicurean source may be found in Philippians 4 and First Timothy 6. In both of these the theme is contentment with little and Paul reveals the origin of his thought by employing Greek words, *autarkes* and *autarkeia,* which are shared with Epicurus and occur only in the Epistles. In this letter to Timothy, Paul writes: "for we brought nothing into the world and we cannot take anything out of it." Epicurus before him had written: "Every man takes leave of life just as he was at the moment of birth."

The same sentiments that endeared the name of Epicurus to multitudes of men in the ancient world have endeared the name of Paul to multitudes of Bible readers in our own times.

Concerning the topic of contentment with little we are informed by Cicero "that no one had more to say about it than Epicurus." He must have discussed it in various writings but all that is left to us, beyond some isolated sayings, is the charming letter to the lad Menoeceus, which his ancient biographer chose for quotation out of more than three hundred rolls. Other affiliations of this letter with Paul's Epistle to Timothy have been mentioned elsewhere in this study, but here it is worth repeating that both letters associate contentment with little with reverence for the divine being and in the letter of Epicurus we find the exhortation that Paul expresses in an identical context of thought in Philippians 4:8: "think on these things."

We shall also gain something by observing that this letter of Epicurus to Menoeceus deserves to rank as the most fascinating specimen extant of the kind of writing known to the Greeks as protreptic, that is, exhortation to the study of philosophy as the guide of life. Now this style of writing, it is needless to say, was indispensable to Christianity as a missionary creed, and Paul alone among the apostles possessed the necessary training for it. All the change that was needed was transposition of his tone to another key, which Paul was amply qualified to make. The protreptic or hortatory tone pervades all his writings and it is expressly designated in this Epistle to Timothy, 6:2: "These things teach and exhort," as it reads in the King James Version.

Thus we observe an attitude, a complex of ideas, and even a terminology that is common to Paul with Epicurus. Each item of this common store, taken by itself, may be discounted as a mere possibility, but the sum of mere possibilities can add up to certainty.

## Authorized Doctrines

The forty Authorized Doctrines of Epicurus constituted the most notorious brief piece of writing in ancient times. Scholars have translated the title in a variety of ways, such as Principal Doctrines, Sovran Maxims, and the like. In this study they are called Authorized Doctrines, partly for the reason that the shrewd judgment of Cicero so appraised them, but chiefly for the reason that the author encouraged his disciples to commit them to memory.

They have been compared to a catechism but more precisely may be designated Articles of Faith. They represent a stage in the development of doctrine which Epicureanism reached as early as 300 B.C., while Christianity was only beginning to arrive at a like stage after 300 A.D. As so often, Epicurus, the pathfinder, had set a precedent.

The Doctrines add up to a mere five pages of print and may easily be perused in twenty minutes; in the form of a roll the bulk would not have exceeded that of a small fountain pen. They were read by friend and foe, by the one for memorization and fond and thoughtful pondering, by the other for derision and refutation. By either standard Paul would have qualified, as a friend in the years of his impulsive adolescence, as a foe in his ardent and consecrated maturity.

Of this notorious collection by far the most notorious were the first four, which declared the master's teachings on the four essentials of the faith: the gods, death, pleasure, and pain. The accident that the number of these was four, combined with the claim of Epicurus to be a healer of souls, prompted some ribald critics to dub them derisively the Tetrapharmacon, which happened to be the name of a popular household remedy compounded of four ingredients: beeswax, resin, pitch, and honey. The name may be rendered Four-in-One but the derisive effect is better reproduced if we say Mrs. Winslow's Soothing Syrup.

Public ridicule, we need not argue, is a tribute to public fame, and our immediate interest in this derided recipe for happiness, the Tetrapharmacon, is to cite it as evidence of what was in the public mind in the time of Paul. If the topics of the gods, death, pleasure, and pain were among the foremost in the public mind, then they were among the foremost in the mind of Paul.

All four of these Authorized Doctrines were highly disturbing to orthodoxy in all its guises. Epicurus may be compared with Charles Darwin and Sigmund Freud in his extraordinary knack for disturbing the public mind. The first Doctrine may have been chosen to head the collection for this very quality. It declares the principle that the divine being is happy itself and makes no business of dispensing troubles to other creatures, that it is not a weak thing and so is not given to anger. This criticism was especially stinging, first to Jews and later to Christians, and had much to do with transforming the God of wrath into the God of love, in which Paul played the foremost role. Although it cannot be claimed that Paul originated the transformation, it is a fact that he rationalized it.

As for the three remaining topics, that of pain has been touched upon in the chapter on Faith, Hope, and Love under the heading of Hope and Health. It will appear again at the end of the present chapter under the heading of Alpha and Omega. The topic of pleasure has been discussed in the chapter on Philippians, while that of death and immortality has been dealt with in the chapter on The Logic of the Cross. As further evidence of Paul's knowledge of the Authorized Doctrines we may consequently turn to the topic of expediency.

174

## Expediency

The term *expedient*, to which the King James Version is partial, has been avoided by the Revised Standard, manifestly for the reason of its having accumulated a load of sinister suggestion, tending to connote the gaining of personal advantage at the expense of another. Both Epicurus and Paul, however, employ the Greek equivalent without scruple or hesitation and for both of them the term denotes the advantage either of the first person or of others. This terminology is virtually technical and admits of no substitution so long as precision of interpretation is the objective, as in the present inquiry. We are consequently calling the topic "expediency."

Two of the chief topics of the Authorized Doctrines are pleasure and justice, concerning which Epicurus makes identical statements: "No pleasure is evil in itself," and "To act unjustly is not an evil in itself." This means that the evil of an action lies solely in the consequences and that the test in either instance is expediency. How this will operate in practice is made clear from a saying of Epicurus taken from another collection: "To all our desires must be applied this question: What will be the result for me if the object of this desire is attained and what if it is not?"

This presumes that the individual is completely at liberty to choose the one or the other and Paul makes this presumption explicit, First Corinthians 6:12: "All things are lawful for me." This rendering, however, is not merely imprecise; it is incorrect. For example, a man is at liberty to steal but this would not be lawful. The meaning is rather: "There is nothing I am not at liberty to do." The principle that Paul asserts is that of free will in man, which Epicurus was the first Greek philosopher to exalt to the eminence of a doctrine. The two men have this in common.

Let us now shift our attention to 10:23 of this same Epistle, where the same principle is twice repeated, "All things are lawful," meaning that the choice between doing or not doing a given thing is always open. The problem in this instance is the eating of meat sacrificed to idols. Such action, Paul would have us believe, in and by itself is quite neutral, neither good nor bad, but, if it causes another to stumble, the factor of evil arises. This evil lies in the consequence, just as Epicurus taught. The test is expediency, which in this case is not selfish but altruistic, consideration for the good of another.

175

Let us now return our attention to the first passage, 6:13, where the problem is that of sexual purity. This is prefaced by the same principle, "All things are lawful," but the test applied in this instance is not expediency; it is given a spiritual guise: "Do you not know that your bodies are members of Christ?" This theme is amplified with Paul's usual adeptness and may be summed up in the statement that the body is "a temple of the Holy Spirit."

In respect of this teaching we are singularly fortunate, because we possess also the teaching of Epicurus worked out in exceptional detail on the principle of expediency. That this teaching in turn had the rank of a classic is evidenced by its inclusion in a collection of Epicurean aphorisms, which, by the way, came to light so recently as 1888 in the Vatican Library. Yet this is not the whole story; additional testimony to the vogue of the teaching in antiquity is a blistering attack upon it by Cicero in a public speech. And if he, speaking far away from Greece in the Roman Forum, was able to count upon an understanding response from jury and spectators to such a blast of satire, may we not with comfortable certainty feel assured that Paul, who in his impressionable youth had been captivated by the siren voices of Epicurus and who was spending his life among the Greeks, was equally familiar with this particular teaching? May we not even infer that he was feeling a challenge to refuse to judge this major offense of impurity by the cold test of expediency and was resolved to institute a new and more fitting test on the higher level of spiritual law?

The teaching of Epicurus has been excerpted from a letter to a correspondent who confessed a proneness to the pleasures of the flesh: "Young man, whenever you are not breaking the laws of the land, nor violating the code of honor sanctioned by good society, nor inflicting wrong upon some neighbor, nor ruining your health, nor squandering your substance, follow your own inclinations just as you please; it is impossible, however, not to become involved in at least one of these offenses, because sexual indulgence never did any good and it is lucky when it does no harm."

That these words were thought worthy to be excerpted and to be enshrined in a collection of aphorisms need not surprise us. They represent the reasoning by expediency at its best, whether it be selfish or altruistic. Epicurus discerns each aspect of the offense: against the state, against society, against the individual neighbor, against health, and against thrift. Paul tacitly brushes them all aside and substitutes a single one, the offense against the Holy Spirit.

It would be undue haste, however, to dismiss the topic at this point; a last scrutiny will be rewarding. We should not, for instance, slip into the error of supposing that motives of expediency are deprived of validity by Paul's substitution of the spiritual sanction. The crux of the question lies in this, that expediency as a motive can never become a satisfactory front for a code of morality. It can never be a cause for pride, unless for an obstinate man such as Epicurus, who dedicated himself to the practice of total honesty. This resoluteness is commendable but it was a chief factor in condemning him to obloquy in the tradition of learning.

Thus expediency as a motive falls into the same class with pleasure as the objective of living; both call for incessant defense and apology. The Stoics chose more prudently, if less courageously. They cherished only such watchwords as called for no apology: virtue, duty, reason, and divine providence. Thus they have fared better than they merited in the tradition of learning; they catered to the unconscious vanity of mankind.

Paul himself is quite capable of putting the spiritual and the expedient on the same level. In Ephesians 6:1 he writes: "Children, obey your parents in the Lord, for this is right." In the very next verse he writes: "Honor your father and your mother" (such is the first commandment with a promise), "that it may be well with you and that you may live long upon the earth." The reward here offered for honor to parents is sheer expediency, selfish advantage.

When Paul quoted the first commandment, it was the orthodox Jew that spoke. When he wrote, "obey your parents in the Lord," it was the regenerate Paul. When he wrote, "All things are lawful," asserting his liberty of choice, it was the ex-Epicurean who spoke. At times it was difficult for him to keep his various personalities in coordination. His mentality operates on the border line between philosophy and religion.

## False Opinions

Paul's knowledge of the Authorized Doctrines is evidenced also by the use of the word *kenodoxia*, which no other writer in the New Testament employs. Mention of this has already been made in the discussion of Galatians 5:26, but some amplification is desirable. The lexicographers and translators have been merely guessing at the meaning of the word. It does not mean "conceit" or "self-conceit." It does not occur in classical Greek and may well have been a coinage of Epicurus. For him it denotes a "false opinion," and what we call an illusion; for example, the idea that rich people are happy. We cannot acquire a clear understanding of it unless we become acquainted with a certain way of reasoning, which originated with Epicurus and was familiar to both Paul and his readers.

This peculiar line of reasoning runs after this fashion. Epicurus thought of the human mind as functioning in two ways: either automatically and unconsciously or consciously and volitionally. For example, it is the automatic mind that takes care of us on our daily rounds, keeping us from tripping over the curb or falling into excavations. This mind, however, is very prone to error. For instance, to quote an ancient example, the boat upon which we are passengers may seem to be in motion and the adjacent boat to be standing still, while the opposite is true. It is the automatic mind that commits the error, which is corrected by the conscious or volitional mind.

A similar type of error is discerned on the ethical level; human beings carelessly allow the flesh to do their thinking for them. To illustrate, in Authorized Doctrine 20 Epicurus writes: "It is the flesh that finds the limits of pleasure to be infinite." The rational mind knows better; it knows that a natural ceiling has been set to the pleasure of eating, that is, the satisfaction of hunger. Again, in Doctrine 30, speaking of hunger and thirst, Epicurus makes the point that the urge to gratify them may be intense but the idea that any real distress will follow if they are not gratified is a "false opinion." The rational mind knows better; the automatic, irrational mind has allowed the flesh to make a decision for it. This is a context in which we find the singular term *kenodoxia*.

Out of this line of reasoning inaugurated by Epicurus arose the antithesis of the flesh to the mind, which preceded the antithesis of the flesh to the Spirit. Paul exhibits undoubtable evidence of his familiarity with the previous phase of the idea, especially in Romans 7:13–25, where he elaborates it. The last verse states this explicitly: "I of myself serve the law of God with my *mind*, but with my *flesh* I serve the law of sin."

In this passage we recognize a stage in the growth of this figure of thought that stands midway between philosophy and religion. The opposition of the flesh to the mind has been unmistakably taken over from philosophy while the concepts of law and sin had their origin in Judaism. The subsequent stage is to be observed in Galatians 5:17: "For the desires of the flesh are against the Spirit, and the desires of the Spirit are against the flesh." The final phase exhibits itself in First Corinthians 2, where the judgments of the mind with its diligent calculus of advantage have been completely superseded by the verdicts of the Spirit, which "judges all things."

## The Deceitfulness of Riches

The affinity of Paul's teachings to those of Epicurus will become still more clear for us if we glance at the topics of fame, power, and riches, especially the last. Those people who thoughtlessly allow their feelings to make their decisions for them are prone to believe that the famous, the powerful, and the rich are happy. These are "false opinions" in the exact sense that Epicurus used that phrase and he campaigned against them just as Jesus and Paul did afterward.

This topic goes more properly with the Gospels, where the material is more abundant, but Paul specifically deals with what is rightly translated in the King James Version "the deceitfulness of riches" and wrongly changed in the Revised Standard to "the delight in riches." Moreover, both his ideology and his terminology reveal unmistakable recollections of known sayings of Epicurus. For instance, the latter writes: "No man looks on evil and deliberately chooses it; but, baited by something that seems good in comparison with an evil greater than itself, he gets trapped." Alongside of this let us place Paul's words in the context already cited, First Timothy 6:9: "But those who desire to be rich fall into temptation, into a trap," and so on.

Yet there is a point to be added from the side of terminology. Epicurus writes: "Human nature is not to be coerced but persuaded, and we shall persuade it by satisfying the necessary desires and the natural desires also, provided only they do not injure us, but relentlessly rejecting the injurious." Paul in the verses quoted in part above goes on to say that those who desire to be rich "fall a prey to many irrational and injurious desires."

In this passage the "irrational desires" are the "false opinions" of Epicurus, dictated by the feelings and not checked by reason. As for "injurious desires," the Greek word for "injurious" is here a solitary occurrence in the New Testament and a favorite of Epicurus.

## Creation and Civilization

Another topic that we know to have been expounded in the Big Epitome was the creation of the world, and Paul's knowledge of this exposition may readily be certified.

At the outset we should not be surprised to learn that the topic was treated by Epicurus with his customary ridicule; it seemed absurd to him to believe that an earth so abounding in uninhabitable wastes of water and mountains, torrid deserts, and regions rigid with cold should have been the creation of a benevolent and all-wise being. He scoffed at the idea that man had been given dominion over the beasts of the field; the world had no more been made for the sake of man than for the sake of insects. Civilization, in his view of things, was the aggregate of the cumulative experience of mankind; all the supremacy enjoyed by man was the fruit of his own labors and pains. In a universe governed by natural laws man alone was an intelligent creature and endowed with freedom of the will.

We also know that the Epicurean procedure in breaking down the beliefs of religion was to ask bantering questions and we possess enough evidence to reconstruct their attacks upon the Book of Genesis. A trivial example from the record may give us a lead: if the sun and the moon were not created until the fourth day, what is the sense of saying "that the evening and the morning were the first day"?

A more important query, however, must claim our attention. Epicurus had attached much importance to the study of infinity and one aspect of this was the problem of time. This study resulted in certain acute reasonings, which were employed by later disciples to embarrass Jews and Christians. These reasonings, as was usual, were cast in the form of bantering questions. For example, they demanded to know: "What was God doing before he created the heaven and earth?"

Even three centuries after Paul's time this question remained so vexatious that St. Augustine dealt with it at great length in his *Confessions* 11:10–31.

Especially vexatious was the implication that God had experienced a change of mind. Recognition of this fact is the key to the interpretation of a clause in James 1:17: "with whom is no variableness, neither shadow of turning." On this point there is regrettable fumbling in the Revised Standard: "with whom there is no variation or *shadow due to change.*" The meaning is clear: with God there is no changing or possibility of changing, neither in the past nor in the future; he was not changing his mind when he became the creator nor will he go back on his promise to glorify mankind. As Paul writes in Hebrews 10:23, "for he who promised is faithful."

With a bit more precision the words of James 1:17 may be rendered: "with whom is no changing or glimmer of defaulting." God will not default on his promise.

Paul, unlike St. Augustine, had no time for argumentation. He retorts to his unnamed questioners dogmatically and declares, in effect, that God had never suffered a change of mind; on the contrary, the exaltation of mankind had been his intention before time began. This retort may be read in First Corinthians 2:7: "But we tell you of wisdom in the form of a mystery revealed, the wisdom that had been hidden, which God preordained in advance of the ages for our glorification."

At this point we should pause to observe that this wisdom which was "preordained in advance of the ages" is divine providence, but the word *providence* is never employed by Paul; in the whole New Testament it occurs but twice and in neither instance has reference to God. In Paul's concept of things the wisdom of God and the providence of God are synonymous and identical; they are inseparable ideas, inseparable in the same sense that God and the love of God are inseparable.

Incidentally, Paul, like Epicurus before him, is addicted to this notion of inseparable ideas. It may be recalled that Epicurus in the fifth of his Authorized Doctrines insisted upon the inseparability of the virtuous life and the happy life. In his ethic they could no more be separated than heat could be separated from fire, whiteness from snow, or sweetness from honey.

It is because of this neat and tidy principle that Paul feels no need to have a separate word for the providence of God. For the very reason that the wisdom of God is "preordained in advance of the ages" it is a blueprint for all future events. Even the course of history and civilization is predetermined. Paul literally believed that the Roman Empire was part of the divine plan; otherwise he could not have written, as he does in Romans 13:1: "The powers that be are ordained of God." Creation and history are inseparable parts of a single plan. Paul not only held that God had created mankind; he also believed that God had mapped off the earth, assigned territory to each race, and determined the length of its tenure, the very dates of history. The supporting text is in Acts 17:26: "And he created from a single beginning every race of men to dwell upon the face of the earth, having fixed the times appointed for them and the bounds of their habitation."

These words were uttered in the hall of the Court of the Areopagus in Athens and, when Paul uttered them, there can be little doubt that his gaze was directed straight into the faces of the mocking Epicurean philosophers, who in the market place previously had asked: "What would this babbler say?" Unless his concept of history had been babble to these "mockers," Paul would never have thrown this pronouncement into their faces so defiantly. As for these men who were being defied, they had learned from the master that the Trojan war, for example, was "an accident of time, place, and persons," that history was the struggle for existence, and civilization the evolution of the unintended.

Paul, however, could also cast a dart of ridicule. To him this Epicurean view of the nature of things was "the wisdom of men," fit only for "children," that is, in his vocabulary, adolescents. The logic of opposites applies here; in First Corinthians 2:6 we read: "We tell of wisdom in an audience of adults."

## Alpha and Omega

A fitting topic for the conclusion of this survey will be the symbolism of alpha and omega, which is familiar to us in its most elaborated form, Revelation 22:13: "I am the Alpha and the Omega, the first and the last, the beginning and the end."

It is somewhat astonishing to discover what a diversity of meanings can be ascribed by learned men to these seemingly simple words. In reality the trail of the truth is easy to follow, provided only the proper clue has once been spotted. This trail leads first to Paul and then to Epicurus. The Pauline reference occurs in Hebrews 12:2, where a certain degree of hesitation is exhibited in the translations. The King James reads: "looking unto Jesus, the author and finisher of our faith," while the Revised Standard essays to improve by reading: "the pioneer and perfecter of our faith."

Both of these versions have the defect of diverting the attention to

182

unessential features of the idea and away from the essentials. The core
of the meaning may be summed up in the statement that the plan of
salvation has its beginning and its end in Jesus the Christ. In order to
apprehend this with clearness we must keep in mind the concept of the
interim, of which the prior limit was the crucifixion and resurrection
of Jesus and the later limit was to be the second coming and the general
resurrection.

In these two events the active agent was Jesus the Christ, delegated
to the task by God the Father. The crucifixion was a voluntary sacrifice and at the event of the second coming the Son will voluntarily restore to the Father the special powers which had been delegated to him,
as we read in First Corinthians 15:24. Thus Christ is "the beginner and
the finisher of our faith." The mistake against which we must be on
guard is to assume that *faith* signifies the Christian religion; this is the
error that leads our recent translators to write: "the pioneer and perfecter of our faith." To Paul the word *faith* signifies the virtue of the
interim, which begins with the first coming and will definitely end with
the second coming. By this event the faith of the believer will have been
justified and terminated.

The trail leads next to Epicurus and our discovery may be startling
at the same time that it adds precision to our understanding. In the
charming but provocative letter to Menoeceus, which Paul manifestly
knew, we find a statement from the pen of Epicurus: "Pleasure is the
beginning and the end of the happy life." To condense the whole meaning of this saying to a single sentence or even a single paragraph would
be impossible, but the gist of it may be briefly paraphrased. Epicurus
conceived of human life as an interim of consciousness bounded by
birth and death. The first act of the newborn child is to reach out for
food, which is a form of pleasure. His last act, providing that he has
lived a life of wisdom, is to take leave of life with a joyous paean of
victory over death, which is also pleasure.

The next step in our reasoning will be to invoke the logic of opposites. When John writes in Revelation, "I am the beginning and the
end," he is tacitly repudiating the rival doctrine, which multitudes
knew by heart: "Pleasure is the beginning and the end of the happy
life." With a critical glance at the Greek original it is even possible to
improve the translation and arrive at a proper emphasis: "It is I who am
the beginning and the end," inviting the informed reader to add, "and

183

not pleasure." We modern readers fail to do this, because the dictum of Epicurus is no longer part of the public mind.

The correctness of this interpretation is confirmed by a detail that may readily be overlooked as lacking particular significance. In close context with the above verse of John in Revelation 22:13 we read that the saints shall enter the City of God by the gates but "without are the dogs, the poisoners, the fornicators," and so on. These dogs are not the animals of the streets, which would be pointless, but Epicureans, who by declaring "that pleasure is the beginning and the end of the happy life," had brought man down to the level of the beasts. The recourse to this gibe is not singular in this passage. We should recall that Paul in Philippians 3:2 had issued the warning, "Beware of the dogs," and in verse 19 made clear the reference to the Epicureans by the words: "Their god is the belly and they glory in their shame."

For Epicurus it was of no avail that he practiced asceticism and restricted the scope of pleasure to the satisfaction of natural and necessary desires. The very name of pleasure meant damnation for him in the eyes of those who feared his doctrines and hated his popularity. To the Christians he was Antichrist.

To return now to Paul, despite the fact that the name of pleasure was repellent to him, the tidy reasonings of Epicurus were to an equal degree attractive. Epicurus, for instance, in the very same paragraph in which he denominates pleasure as "the beginning and the end of the happy life," lays down the principle that sometimes we deliberately choose to endure pain for the sake of a subsequent pleasure that outweighs the pain. Paul, in his turn, in the very same sentence of Hebrews 12:2, where he tacitly scorns pleasure as "the beginning and the end of the happy life" and hails Jesus instead as "the beginner and the finisher of our faith," makes this momentous addition: "who for the joy that was set before him endured the cross."

This plainly exemplifies the sober formula of Epicurus, that the pain is deliberately chosen for the sake of the pleasure that outweighs it, but with what a difference! A studied formula of everyday morality, activated by expediency, has been lifted out of the earthly code of conduct in which it was conceived, raised to the spiritual level of experience, and endowed with a meaningfulness of which it had seemed incapable.

Appendix and Indexes

# APPENDIX

T HE teachings of Epicurus were well known to Paul and to multitudes of people in his day. A few of the more outstanding examples are here appended.

The first of these deals with the divine nature and was long vexatious to Christians on account of its tacit criticism of "the wrath of God."

Authorized Doctrine 1: "The blessed and incorruptible being neither knows tribulation itself nor occasions it to another; it is consequently immune to feelings of either anger or gratitude, for all such emotion signifies a weak creature."

The second example deals with the topic of death and by the force of repulsion furnished much of the inspiration for Paul's eloquent exposition of the new immortality in First Corinthians 15.

Authorized Doctrine 2: "Death is nothing to us, because dissolution means unconsciousness and unconsciousness is nothing to us."

## Peace and Safety

In Second Thessalonians 5:3 Paul identifies the Epicureans by the words "Peace and Safety." The extent to which the mind of Epicurus was preoccupied by this topic is made clear by the following extracts.

Quoted by Plutarch: "Live and die unknown." Epicurus means that the obscure life is the safest.

Authorized Doctrine 6: "Political rule and kingly power being what they are, it is a good thing to feel secure in human relations no matter through whose agency one is able to attain this."

Authorized Doctrine 7: "Some men wish to gain reputation and to be in the public eye, thinking by this means to win security from the attacks of men. Consequently, if the lives of these men are safe they have achieved the end ordained by Nature; if, on the contrary, their lives are not safe they lack that for which at the outset they reached out in obedience to an instinct of Nature."

Authorized Doctrine 13: "It is of no avail to have established security in human relations if things above and in the earth beneath and those in the infinite universe in general are viewed with uncertainty."

Authorized Doctrine 14: "Even though security from the injuries of men may have been established to a certain degree by dynastic protection, the most unalloyed feeling of security is to be found in the retired life and withdrawal from the multitude."

Authorized Doctrine 17: "Of all the preparations that wisdom makes for the blessedness of the perfect life, by far the most important is the acquisition of friendship."

Authorized Doctrine 18: "The same conviction that makes us feel confident of nothing terrible being either eternal or even of long duration discerns the assurance of safety within the narrow limits of this life itself as being most perfectly effected by friendship."

Authorized Doctrine 39: "That man has best established the feeling of security from external hazards who has made his relationships friendly wherever possible; where this has been impossible has made them at least not unfriendly; and wherever even this has been impossible avoids contacts; and wherever it paid him to do so has arranged dynastic protection."

## The Letter to Menoeceus

Paul shows himself familiar with the letter to Menoeceus, which is the best specimen extant of the writings of Epicurus. It belongs in the class known as protreptic or hortatory, urging the study of philosophy as the guide of life. It was no more intended for the exclusive instruction of Menoeceus than the Epistles to Timothy were intended for his exclusive use.

### Epicurus to Menoeceus: Greetings.

"Let no one delay to philosophize while he is young nor weary in philosophizing when he is old, for no one is either short of the age or past the age for enjoying health of the soul. And the man who says the time for philosophizing has not yet come or is already past may be compared to the man who says the time for happiness is not yet come or is already gone by. So both the young man and the old man should philosophize, the former that while growing old he may be young in blessings because of gratitude for what has been, the latter that he may be young and old at the same time because of the fearlessness with which he faces the future. Therefore the wise plan is to practice the things that make for happiness, since possessing happiness we have everything and not possessing it we do everything to have it.

### THE GODS

"Both practice and study the precepts which I continuously urged upon you, discerning these to be the A B C's of the good life. First of all, believing the divine being to be blessed and incorruptible, just as the universal idea of it is outlined in our minds, associate nothing with it that is incompatible with incorruption or alien to blessedness. And cultivate every thought concerning it that can preserve its blessedness along with incorruption. Because there are gods, for the knowledge of them is plain to see. They are not, however, such as many suppose them to be, for people do not keep their accounts of them consistent with their beliefs. And it is not the man who would abolish the gods of the multitude who is impious but the man who associates the beliefs of the multitude with the gods; for the pronouncements of the multitude concerning the gods are not innate ideas but false assumptions. According to their stories the greatest injuries and indignities are said to be inflicted upon evil men, and also benefits.

### THE GODS INDIFFERENT TO WICKEDNESS

"[These stories are false, because the gods], being exclusively devoted to virtues that become themselves, feel an affinity for those like themselves and regard all that is not of this kind as alien.

### DEATH

"Habituate yourself to the belief that death is nothing to us, because all good and evil lies in consciousness and death is the loss of consciousness. Hence a right understanding of the fact that death is nothing to us renders enjoyable the mortality of life, not by adding infinite time but by taking away the yearning for immortality, for there is nothing to be feared while living by the man who has genuinely grasped the idea that there is nothing to be feared when not living.

So the man is silly who says that he fears death, not because it will pain him when it comes, but because it pains him in prospect; for nothing that occasions no trouble when present has any right to pain us in anticipation. Therefore death, the most frightening of evils, is nothing to us, for the excellent reason that while we live it is not here and when it is here we are not living. So it is nothing either to the living or to the dead, because it is of no concern to the living and the dead are no longer.

### THE INCONSISTENCY OF PEOPLE

"But the multitude of men at one time shun death as the greatest of evils and at another choose death as an escape from the evils of life. The wise man, however, neither asks quarter of life nor has he any fear of not living, for he has no fault to find with life nor does he think it any evil to be out of it. Just as in the case of food, he does not always choose the largest portion but rather the most enjoyable; so with time, he does not pick the longest span of it but the most enjoyable.

"And the one who bids the young man 'Live well' and the old man 'Die well' is simple-minded, not only because of the pleasure of being alive, but also for the reason that the art of living well and dying well is one and the same. And far worse is he who says: 'It were well never to have been born or having been born to have passed with all speed through the gates of Hades.' For if he is saying this out of conviction, why does he not take leave of life? Because this course is open to him if he has resolutely made up his mind to it. But if he is speaking in mockery, he is trifling in the case of things that do not countenance trifling.

### THE FUTURE

"As for the future, we must bear in mind that it is not quite beyond our control nor yet quite within our control, so that we must neither await it as going to be quite within our control nor despair of it as going to be quite beyond our control.

### THE DESIRES

"As for the desires, we should reflect that some are natural and some are imaginary; and of the natural desires some are necessary and some are natural only; and of the necessary desires some are necessary to happiness [he refers to friendship], and others to the comfort of the body [clothing and housing], and others to life itself [hunger and thirst].

"Because a correct appraisal of the desires enables us to refer every decision to choose or to avoid to the test of the health of the body and the tranquillity of the soul, for this is the objective of the happy life. For to this end we do everything, that we may feel neither pain nor fear. When once this boon is in our possession, every tumult of the soul is stilled, the creature having nothing to work forward to as something lacking or something additional to seek whereby the good of the soul and the body shall arrive at fullness. For only then have we need of pleasure when from the absence of pleasure we feel pain; and conversely, when we no longer feel pain we no longer feel need of pleasure.

### THE BEGINNING AND THE END OF THE HAPPY LIFE

"And for the following reason we say that pleasure is the beginning and the end of the happy life: because we recognize pleasure as the first good and connate with us and to this we have recourse as to a canon, judging every good by the reaction. And for the reason that pleasure is the first good and of one nature with us we do not choose every pleasure but at one time or another forgo many pleasures when a distress that will outweigh them follows in consequence of these pleasures; and many pains we believe to be preferable to pleasures when a pleasure that will outweigh them ensues for us after enduring those pains for a long time. Therefore every pleasure is good because it is of one nature with us but every pleasure is not to be chosen; by the same reasoning every pain is an evil but every pain is not such as to be avoided at all times.

### EXPEDIENCY: THE CALCULUS OF ADVANTAGE

"The right procedure, however, is to weigh them against one another and to scrutinize the advantages and disadvantages; for we treat the good under certain circumstances as an evil and conversely the evil as a good.

### SELF-SUFFICIENCY OR CONTENTMENT WITH LITTLE

"And self-sufficiency we believe to be a great good, not that we may live on little under all circumstances but that we may be content with little when we do not have plenty, being genuinely convinced that they enjoy luxury most who feel the least need of it; that every natural appetite is easily gratified but the unnatural appetite difficult to gratify; and that plain foods bring a pleasure equal to that of a luxurious diet when all the pain originating in need has been removed; and that bread and water bring the most utter pleasure when one in need of them brings them to his lips.

"Thus habituation to simple and inexpensive diets not only contributes to perfect health but also renders a man unshrinking in face of the inevitable emergencies of life; and it disposes us better toward the times of abundance that ensue after intervals of scarcity and renders us fearless in the face of Fortune. When therefore we say that pleasure is the end we do not mean the pleasures of profligates and those that consist in high living, as certain people think, either not understanding us and holding to different views or willfully misrepresenting us; but we mean freedom from pain in the body and turmoil in the soul. For it is not protracted drinking bouts and revels nor yet sexual pleasures with boys and women nor rare dishes of fish and the rest — all the delicacies that the luxurious table bears — that beget the happy life but rather sober calculation, which searches out the reasons for every choice and avoidance and expels the false opinions, the source of most of the turmoil that seizes upon the souls of men.

### THE PRACTICAL REASON

"Of all these virtues the source is the practical reason, the greatest good of all — and hence more precious than philosophy itself — teaching us the impossibility of living pleasurably without living according to reason, honor, and justice, and conversely, of living according to reason, honor, and justice without living pleasurably; for the virtues are of one nature with the pleasurable life and conversely, the pleasurable life is inseparable from the virtues.

### DESCRIPTION OF THE HAPPY MAN

"Because who do you think is in better case than the man who holds pious beliefs concerning the gods and is invariably fearless of death; and has included in his reckoning the end of life as ordained by Nature; and concerning the utmost of things good discerns this to be easy to enjoy to the full and easy of procurement, while the utmost of things evil is either brief in duration or brief in suffering.

"He has abolished the Necessity that is introduced by some thinkers as the mistress of all things, for it were better to subscribe to the myths concerning the gods than to be a slave to the Destiny of the physicists, because the former presumes a hope of mercy through worship but the latter assumes Necessity to be inexorable.

"As for Fortune, he does not assume that she is a goddess, as the multitude believes, for nothing is done at random by a god; neither does he think her a fickle cause, for he does not suppose that either good or evil is dealt out to men by her to affect life's happiness; yet he does believe the starting points for great good or evil to originate with her, thinking it better to plan well and fail than to plan badly and succeed, for in the conduct of life it profits more for good judgment to miscarry than for misjudgment to prosper by chance.

### THINK ON THESE THINGS

"Meditate therefore by day and by night upon these precepts and upon the others that go with these, whether by yourself or in the company of another like yourself, and never will your soul be in turmoil either sleeping or waking but you will be living like a god among men, for in no wise does a man resemble a mortal creature who lives among immortal blessings."

# Verses Newly Explained or Translated

194

# Words and Topics